DEVELOPING THE SELF

Developing the Self

Through the Inner Work Path
in the Light of Anthroposophy

LISA ROMERO

SteinerBooks | 2015

SteinerBooks
An imprint of Anthroposophic Press, Inc.
610 Main Street, Great Barrington, MA 01230
SteinerBooks.org

Library of Congress Cataloging-in-Publication-data
is available on request.

PRINT: 978-1-62148-123-2
eBook: 978-1-62148-124-9

Contents

INTRODUCTION

Our inner lives need strengthening to continue to evolve healthfully through the intense challenges that life is presenting us with. We are not to flee from these challenges, but meet them because it is only in meeting them that we continue to strengthen and transform. Our path through the world is indeed a guided one, but in the clamor of life it is hard to receive these insights of guidance. The inner work helps us to help ourselves, to develop capacities and to become aware of our guiding forces and open to them.

External life will become increasingly complicated; that cannot be prevented. But souls will find the way to one another through a deepened inner life.

> Outer laws and institutions will make life so complicated that people may well lose their bearings altogether. But by realizing the truth of the law of Karma, the knowledge will be born in the soul of what it must do in order to find from within, its path through the world.[1]

This small book begins at a different entry point than the meditative practice. It enters into the living reality of needing to take hold of ourselves and transform ourselves in daily life. Being aware of the great journey that the human being travels, we can find our place and how our task serves us to work onward. The first chapter is an overview and direction; it may seem full, but the points are met again in the following chapters, where the life experience is addressed.

I have worked with hundreds of teachers in the last twenty years. I have chosen to do this work because of the important role they play in preparing a ground for children that will assist their path of self-development when they have become adults. It is through our understanding of children that we realize we must live the ways of anthroposophy, not just preach them. Through these teachers I have learned at the same time that portions of the inner work path need to be very practical, understandable, and more meaningful for their lives. Inner work should be relevant to the tasks we have to carry out in the world, rather than separated from the tasks that we must focus our time and energy on.

In the second chapter, we see how this essential work of supporting child development not only helps us to understand the child's needs, but also supports in reflecting on our own path and how we came to where we are now. "People who relate only to the body cannot grow younger, for their souls will share in everything the body experiences. Of course it will not be possible to change the habit of going grey; but it is possible for a grey head to gain a young soul from the wellspring of spiritual life."[2]

The collection of exercises in the third chapter is not intended to overwhelm the reader, but to express the path more clearly. As the book is read, the reader will see that through self-evaluation and self-discernment there are certain types of exercises that will be most productive for each person. In our times when so much is offered, it is important to know what we are doing, why we are doing it, and what results it would lead to. These few chapters will help to shine the light on how to evaluate which capacities need to be developed; how to develop them; and what exercises are useful to assist transformation.

This book is intended to be useful for people at all levels of inner development. The last chapter focuses on the preparation for the initiation of the I. By seeing a larger picture we can recognize how the exercises we do today relate to all that we are working toward. What we are doing now not only supports our life now, but also will become the ground for the highest spiritual work in the future.

As we enter more deeply into the consciousness soul age, we will need to find the supports and the capacities to overcome the necessary difficulties this age presents us with. We are struck with difficulties regardless of how far we have traveled. "Every single soul has difficulties to encounter because the consciousness soul can develop only through the testing occasioned by the overcoming of these difficulties."[3]

When writing the first book (*The Inner Work Path: A Foundation of Meditative Practice in the Light of Anthroposophy*), I was aware that it was but a small part; always more can be said and given. This book serves to complement the first, even though each can stand alone. It does not retread the meditative form, but illuminates the living reality of our self in relationship to the world. Therefore, the exercises presented here are for the living daily inner work through self-development and contemplation. This material assists both meditants and non-meditants alike.

We really do justice to the inner path only when it is lived into the outer world. In our intellectual cleverness we can speak of all things spiritual; we can even understand intellectually the great teachers, and speak as though their words are our words. We may attend to our meditations daily, and turn up for the important esoteric lessons. But without taking hold of how we live in the world through what lives in our own being, we really only serve ourselves. Many people drawn to these paths wish to gain more personal selfness, more "me self." The inner work path asks for us to transform who we are as a way to genuine knowledge, not merely to accumulate others' insights. In fact, it can be a greater fall to know the truth in our thinking and yet live the error in the sphere of life. We are asked to live what we know; yet we all fall short of this because we all know more than we can live. The inner work path of self-development guides us to the understanding of the essential task of living the inner work. It provides us the reasoning, exercises, and results of transforming the particular self toward the greater self, the spirit being.

BODY, MIND, AND SPIRIT

Having an understanding of how the human being develops and evolves in each aspect of self allows insight into every stage of human growth. There is the growth of the outer body, the development of the mind, and the awakening awareness of the spirit, of the true self. Before we enter into the detail of each of these in the following chapters, it is useful to describe the overview of their evolution from the point of view of one aspect of esotericism and its terminology.

The Body

The growth of the body we see as a fact of life, observable and quantifiable. Every child will need to reach definite milestones, such as the change of teeth and puberty. Even if the milestones are achieved at different ages, or with different levels of ease or struggle, they still need to be achieved if the body is to grow into adulthood.

In the light of anthroposophy, the outer comprises three definable sheaths. First, the physical body, which is the mineral outer form and shape; it places the human being in space. The physical body begins to develop independently from the mother at birth. Second, the etheric body, which enables growth and life; as in the plant world, it is the vehicle of time and the life processes. The etheric body begins to develop independently at the change of teeth. Third, the sensitivity organization, which is called the sentient body; it gives rise to sensation and bodily experience from both outer and inner stimuli. It becomes independent at puberty.

These sheaths take their substance from the outer world. The physical body is the chemistry and matter that can be observed, dissected, and related to substances that we find in the outer world. The etheric body carries the hereditary impulses passed on through the generations. As the signature of the life processes, it will determine tendencies toward illnesses and strengths in the bodily vehicle. The sentient body is formed throughout its development by interaction with the sense world and is affected by that world. It is differentiated depending on the sensory stimulation, environmental stressors, and impressions that affect the sensing quality of the sentient body. The three bodies together form our biological drive. These cause the human being to survive both individually, by way of basic needs for shelter and food, and collectively, through our procreative force and the need to reproduce and bond. We have this physical part of the human being in common with the animal kingdom.

All three bodily sheaths grow through time and in space until the adult form and vehicle for the inner being has emerged. We recognize that to reach adulthood and become a grown citizen of the earthly world these bodies need to grow. The conditions of time and space that belong to the outer world and the physical laws that govern life on earth hold sway in these bodies, but there are other effects that come from the inner being of the individual, which also leave their imprint on the condition of this vehicle.

The Mind

The human being also has a complex mind or inner life. We recognize our inner life changing, developing capacities as we experience various life events. These events range from everyday life experience to unusual encounters that are unique to our individual biography. The inner human being or mind is termed the "soul" in anthroposophy. The soul is sometimes called the astral body because it is the vehicle for soul activity and the expression of the soul experiences. Along with the sentient body, which registers the stimuli, the astral body comprises all three soul processes or three inner activities. In anthroposophy they are called the sentient soul, the intellectual soul, and the consciousness soul. In other spiritual teachings, they have also been named the instinctual mind, the reasoning mind, and the discerning mind.

The sentient soul or instinctual mind is the part of our inner life that has liking and disliking, feeling sympathy and antipathy toward the experiences that meet us. Seeking pleasure and avoiding pain according to these sympathies or antipathies is a strong part of the activity of the sentient soul. It is the soul body of desires and passions, of cravings and longings. It fuels our need for ambition, and it drives us. It moves us to fulfill everything from the basic biological drives to our more complex needs, such as the need for approval. Often seeking to fulfill patterns of reward that have been instilled by childhood experiences, its primary need is to gratify the longings and hunger within. It also wants things like justice and rights; but generally desires them for itself. The inner sentient soul connects to the outer body through the sensitivity organization or sentient body.

As we develop as adults, we can begin to feel the instinctual mind or sentient soul as our less-developed self. When we feel emotional, driven, and reactive to life events, we don't feel in control. The sentient soul is like a demanding and compelling force within, which is stronger or weaker depending on the individual. We often don't like this side of ourselves, especially if we have an inner battle between cravings and our rational decisions. For example we may decide to eat more healthfully, and yet cravings and desires can compel us to eat the food that we have decided is not beneficial for us. At the same time, if we suppress the forces arising from our sentient soul we often feel we have shutdown our passion and energy for life. In the sentient soul also live passion and vibrancy, fueling the love of life in the sense world. It is the sentient soul that can live life as a gathering place of experience, free from the shoulds and should-nots of conditioning imposed from outside itself.

The intellectual soul or reasoning mind allows us to think through our experiences and rationalize our choices and decisions. We can also override a desire that may not, with our thinking, seem healthy or acceptable for us. We can have insight and understanding for ourselves, feeling into what we are and what we want to become. We can do things we do not desire to do because we wish to gain other outcomes. The scientific approach makes use of the intellectual soul. It is the soul body of thinking and reasoning, of connecting thoughts, and working things through logically and rationally according to the information we have.

We do not, however, necessarily think through every thought we have to consciously worked conclusions; rather, in our thinking we operate with many conditioned thought processes. Once we have learned a particular pathway and conclusion in our thinking, we do not think it through each time. This tendency is very valuable when accessing such things as mathematics, where it is not necessary to learn each time anew that the three angles of a triangle make 180°. Once something is learned, it becomes the scaffolding in our thinking that can allow us to have deeper thoughts. Every time we read, we don't need to relearn the letters and words.

In childhood as this intellectual soul is being inscribed upon, it is very susceptible to all sorts of impressions. We are able to belong to the collective through learning the social norms and values. Certain impressions are necessary to live in this world, and are verifiable norms of thinking and appraising the world. In contrast, other thoughts are conditioning that is passed on through others—thoughts we are told to have—and these in turn become our beliefs.

If children have been taught certain religious beliefs by their family and community, they may never question these; instead, they take them as given fact, just as the triangle is a given fact. Likewise, much conditioning that we receive from our community is one-sided and therefore indoctrinates us, impressing one-sided beliefs. The individual child has no choice in this matter of conditioning because the inner intellectual soul connects to the outer body via the etheric body, the body of heredity and community. The adult may choose to think through the concepts instilled in childhood, and may also conclude that they are true; but more often such thoughts are not even considered as conditioned concepts, only as facts. The intellectual soul is enriched through learning and experiencing both consciously and unconsciously. Therefore, we do not always know what we believe until our beliefs are challenged.

Many people in the western culture tend toward a preference for the more objective, rational, intellectual soul that can reason, and makes sense of others' behavior and the world around them. The mass consciousness of humanity regards this intelligence as the civilized, educated mind. When the intellectual soul is most at work, we can experience a detachment from the effects of the world around us, and look on with a scientific eye at any given situation. We gain clarity and feel in control, and therefore many may think of this as our preferred or better selves.

The consciousness soul, or discerning mind, works in the inner life to give an awareness of self, a recognition of self that also determines how we live and stand in a foundational way in the outer world. This activity can override the reasoning of the intellectual soul. From a place of inner knowing and surety we may act upon something not out of desire, not even out of reasoning, but out of knowing that it is right; that it must be done. The consciousness soul also has the possibility of being our individual moral compass. This gives us a core experience of selfness that we feel is our individual being and knowing.

When all the desires and passions and conditions have gone, when there is no more thought or content in the mind, we still experience a presence, a consciousness. Many would regard this as an experience of their true self. Yet this consciousness is still bound with this individual body, this individual life. When all is quieted, and without thoughts or content, there is continual relatedness in time and space to the individual body. The consciousness soul connects to the outer body through the physical sheath.

The consciousness soul or discerning mind is often experienced as the central self, the connected self. We find this in moments of contemplation, and can develop this connectedness through taking time for reflection. Often we connect with this soul aspect only when we are alone. In this aspect of soul we may feel a certain sense of independence, of self-governing. Some may like this, because it may be experienced as a sense of being able to carry things alone and rely on oneself. In contrast, some may not like and may even fear the aloneness. It is in the consciousness soul that the individual spirit lights up most clearly.

All three are required for a healthy and full outer life, as well as a developed inner life. We can evaluate our outer capacities by recognizing which of the soul sheaths tend to dominate during everyday life. This is where we feel ourselves oriented most frequently, and are often (but not always) most comfortable.

In life, the three soul sheaths work as a bridge between the external world of the sense perceptions and our internal world. If we follow an exercise such as observing a living plant and a dying plant, then we can see the bridging activity of the three soul sheaths.

We stand before both a living, growing, flourishing plant and a dying, decaying plant. The sentient soul extends in interest toward the outer, the living or the dying plant. As we place our attention on the plant and at the same time on our inner life, we can have an experience of the plant inwardly. The living plant creates an inner experience of expansion, whereas the dying plant creates an inner experience of contraction. The inner expression of each activity is recalled by the intellectual soul and compared in order to differentiate between our two inner experiences of the plant. The consciousness soul must stay attentive, present, and focused, immersed in the exercise of uniting self with the other (the plant) without losing consciousness of the self.

The soul makes a bridge from the outer sense world toward inner experience; we may call this our own experience. This grows to become our own knowledge of things. We have knowledge of the other through the bridge of the soul. In order to know something, the sentient soul must unite or at least be interested in the other to extend toward it. The intellectual soul must be free of limitations to allow the other to imprint upon it. The consciousness soul must be directed and active in its direction, keeping awareness of self. This process is different from memorizing information or learning through the intellect alone.

When the soul is engaged in this way, it works as an organ of transmission for the spirit within. The spirit is the director of the soul in these schooling exercises. The soul, temporarily liberated from the particular self, opens to the world. This gesture is required for the student of inner work; and if we can live in this way we learn from everything in life.

Much of the time in daily life the soul determines its own direction by following the things that we like and avoiding the things we dislike, usually according to past experiences. Both sympathy and antipathy call the sentient soul to enter into relationship with the outer world, but they do not necessarily lead to learning.

In inner schooling we are given certain exercises like the plant exercise because of the value in understanding the processes in living and dying. We often walk through the world indifferent to all the impressions that are possible; we interact only with the ones that the sentient soul already has some sympathy or antipathy toward. In this way, our particular self governs what we are interested in. What we can learn is therefore limited.

The intellectual soul may block learning because of pre-formed beliefs and assumptions, judging the present out of past known beliefs. If we wish to know the truth of something, we must put our beliefs to one side, or they will color our experience.

The consciousness soul blocks learning by lack of presence with the self, or by lack of connection to what is unfamiliar to our particular self. This block limits what we can know, and what we gain knowledge of, because we do not hold the direction long enough for the connection to grow.

Through inner schooling we are directed to gain knowledge of the essential things that will bring about a contribution to our inner library. We learn not out of preference, but through the will to grow toward the living knowledge of things in the outer world—things that will be necessary to know for further development.

The great gift of this gesture toward learning is described in *Light on the Path*:

In time you will need no teacher. For as the individual has voice, so has that in which the individual exists. Life itself has speech and is never silent. And its utterance is not as you that are deaf may suppose, a cry; it is a song, learn from it that you are part of the harmony; learn from it to obey the laws of the harmony.[4]

All that appears in life can be a glorious learning. Behind all that appears to the senses is an activity creating a movement, rhythm, or pulse that we experience in our inner life. We no longer perceive only the outer form of a thing, but also experience its effects in our soul. These effects arise as an inner movement. What creates this inner changing, streaming within, is not our reaction of liking or not liking what is observed; rather, it is the activity unseen by the eye that lives in the thing itself.

We see the outer thing with our outer senses; we experience the effects with our soul senses; and we recognize the expression of various consciousnesses through our consciousness. The soul can begin to delight in the wonders of the sense world. Hafiz expresses it well:

I have come into the world to hear this: every song
the Earth has sung since it was conceived in the divine womb
and began spinning from His wish, every song by wing
and fin and hoof, every song by heel and tree and woman
    and child;
every song of stream and rock, every song of tool and
    lyre and flute,
every song of gold and emerald and fire
every song the heart should cry with magnificent dignity
    to know itself as God;
for all other knowledge will leave us again in want and
aching – only imbibing the glorious sun will complete us.[5]

All things that present to the outer senses have an effect on the soul. If we give the time to follow the effects, we will experience this for ourselves. However, apart from our own subjective blocks, we may have strengths or weaknesses in the three soul sheaths that prevent them from acting as a clear bridge.

There are several ways in which we can ascertain our individual dominance or weakness in one or more of these three soul sheaths. One way is by observing how well we can achieve the different inner soul strengthening tasks that are given by the inner schooling. Starting with a basic exercise such as the concentration exercise, we can watch our capacities at work and evaluate them.[6] What is easy? Or difficult? What needs developing? What is one-sided?

In this exercise we hold the image of a human-made object such as a pencil in our minds. We try to see the pencil visually, inwardly; and also we have thoughts about the pencil for about five minutes: thoughts about its size, the materials it was made from, and so forth. The important thing is that the logical sequence is decided and ordered by you each time in a living way.

In our capacity to see the pencil we can perceive an activity of our sentient soul. Can we imagine the pencil with inner clarity? Or is it very difficult for us to see it inwardly? Does the pencil look exactly as we want it to look? Or is it moving, changing color or shape, or turning into something completely different?

When the sentient soul is inwardly liberated and ordered, then we inwardly see the pencil clearly. If the sentient soul is underactive, we cannot inwardly image the pencil; if it is overactive or ungoverned, the pencil does not do as we want, as we will it to do.

The thoughts about the pencil that we create in an ordered reasoning manner, in logical sequence, are the activity of the intellectual soul. If we are unable to hold to a logical sequence; or if the mind kaleidoscopes with a question like "I wonder where all the pencils have gone?" or a distracting thought like "I remember my grandfather with a pencil behind his ear," then we have a weakness in our intellectual soul capacity. We need to bring in more form and not allow the mind to wander or fantasize. We also have a weakness in our intellectual soul capacity if we hold a regimented sequence of thoughts that we produce in an unliving manner whenever we do the pencil exercise. In this case, we need to bring living interest into the exercise to override the habit of thinking from the past.

The presence of the consciousness soul is ascertained by our ability to stay focused and concentrated on the exercise regardless of distractions. When there is a lack of capacity we will find our minds going elsewhere, and we have to keep bringing ourselves back to the theme of the exercise. It is useful to witness where the mind strays. Is it to everyday life and concerns? Or is it on a fantasy flight? Another lack of capacity shows itself when the will is so forceful that we drive the pencil exercise in such a way that our hard will forces dominate. We feel we are not freely doing our exercises but are forcefully doing them, causing tension. This personal push of will is different from the free will that we are trying to engage. Learning to surrender our personal hard will by allowing more living activity into the exercise can help to soften our drive.

We can look at all of our meditative or inner development exercises in this light and observe where our strengths and weaknesses lie, and how we can then work toward balancing the one-sidedness of each of these three soul sheaths.

Separating the three soul forces during our exercises, observing them independently of each other, teaches us many things. We may not have clarity around each of these soul aspects of the human being during daily life, because invariably they work as one, and not as three defined forces. However, we have all experienced that through life our capacities can evolve; that there is more soul depth, more soul richness, and our minds have expanded. Through our experiences of life and the way we encounter them, the mind is expanded, and the soul is developed.

The Spirit

The individual spirit is a spark of freedom. It is only through the spirit that we can become free in the true sense of the word. The spirit expressed in life is our conscious individual will. It does not come into full expression until its birth at around nineteen to twenty-one years of age. Many sixteen- to eighteen-year-olds have asked me how they can develop their will, for they recognize it is not in their hands. As much as they want to do certain things, their will is not able to form within them. They feel confined to the will instilled in them as they were growing. Although the individual will, the spark of freedom, may be born at around nineteen years of age, it is dominated by the body and soul patterns until it has taken hold of them. These patterns are our un-freedom and need to be awakened before we can transform them into the fuel of freedom.

Following the drives of the physical body is not freedom. Even when someone says, "I want to have sex with who I want, when I want," if this desire is driven by biological processes such as the millions of sperm wanting to seed the world (the millions of cheerleaders shouting to get outside the body), this is not individual freedom. To put it crudely, it is not my will but my "willy" that draws me or forces an action. An individual man does not have commitment issues, but his biology does. The female body is not seeking to seed the world in the same way, but the ovum is seeking the "right one" to be with. Seeking Mister Right is a biological drive that many think is their individual free expression. These biological drives affect our inner life because they are deeply connected as long as the soul is body-bound. Because of this we can be under the illusion that it is our individual freedom we are acting on, when in fact it is one of our greatest unfreedoms, to be dictated to by the male or female body.

Finding freedom over our biology is difficult. This is the reason fasting can have a positive effect on the power of the individual over the biological drives. Done in a healthy and safe way, fasting places the will-inspired soul over the patterns of the physical. The patterns of the body are often fueled through receiving familiar hormonal and chemical rewards by repeating the patterns the body has become attached to. Through certain food substances and behaviors, we are constantly triggering familiar chemical responses. Withholding normal behavior can awaken the soul activity over the body, through the individual will, potentially freeing the soul from being dictated to by its biology.

We are also unfree when we follow blindly the etheric conditioning of our family, community, race, or religion. We are unfree when we follow blindly the conditioning from either our gender or social standing. When you meet someone, do you bring the same self to that meeting, whether the person is a man or a woman? Or do you adapt and change what you bring or how you bring it, not because the individual circumstances call for it, but because your conditioning is at work? It may not be outwardly obvious; you probably don't start flicking your hair back and flirting, or buffing up your muscles. The conditioning is far more subtle than that. It is as though we bring different aspects of our inner life to the foreground or background, producing varying finer responses according to the gender of the person who is in front of us.

When you speak with a receptionist do you bring your same self to that meeting as you do when you speak with a doctor? Do you hold the same quality of listening, of connecting? We like to think we would be equally as respectful to both the doctor and the receptionist; and perhaps outwardly we are, but we need to follow the deeper changes that take place. If at one of these times you follow the inner changes that take place, the differing attention and the assumptions, you may recognize that your conditioning around social standing creates an unseen lack of freedom.

It is the same for conditions around race and religion. The unseen lack of freedom can feel as if it is our own thought-through conclusion. However, the work of indoctrination runs below the threshold of consciousness. Liberating ourselves from this takes mighty effort.

We are also unfree when we respond to the present moment out of the past; for instance, out of our past biography or our past conditioning. We live out of our past far more than we imagine. Our thinking, our feeling, and our actions are so often operated by the puppet-master of our past. Although it goes unrecognized, we live in a delusion of freedom. We live in an illusion of individual choice, of self-will. If we enquire into much of what we think, feel, and do, we will see that we live on automatic pilot much of the time, and that our automatic pilot works entirely out of our past.

None of this is a conscious activity of the I, but an activity of the collection of conditions we have come to call "I." Whenever we are unconsciously engaged in the world we act out of thousands of conditionings that we carry around with us. Even when we have consciously walked the path of self-development and have developed a capacity to work out of inner freedom, if we do not work actively, then the automatic pilot takes control again. The following poem by Hafiz can be a helpful reminder.

> It is always a danger
> to aspirants on the path
> when they begin to believe
> and act
> as if the ten thousand idiots
> who so long ruled and lived inside
> have all packed their bags
> and skipped town or died.[7]

The spiritual aspect of the individual being has many names. It is named as the I, or as the Ego; sometimes as the true self or the eternal self, perhaps the essential self.

It is that divine spark, the seeming God within. However, the human I has two aspects that need to be recognized as being distinct from each other because they work in opposite directions. First, there is the "sheath I" that in anthroposophy is most commonly called the "ego." Second, there is the "higher I," the fifth member of our being that we currently could be aware of; although, because of our condition of being bound to the outer world, we may not recognize this fifth member. Through the higher I we can become participators in the spiritual world.

Esoteric pupils should free themselves from all external influences surrounding them, not in order to flee the world but rather in order to make independent their own true higher I, the spiritual self, the true human being within. In truth we have not just four but five members; namely, the physical body, the etheric body, the astral body, and the sheath I, behind which is found the true I—the actual I, the true human being.[8]

The true I lives hidden within human consciousness. It remains hidden until, through soul development, it has gained strength and stature. Liberating the soul from its state of being body-bound awakens the true I. Once the soul is liberated, it can turn toward the spirit and recognize the I as the true being. It then may place its powers in service to what is higher within. Until then the I remains shrouded within, yet active without, creating the life experiences that will eventually awaken the soul to the presence of itself, the true I.

Until this awakening, we operate primarily out of the sheath I, the ego; this is, for many, our individual identity.

The ego can be the core of selfness that acts like the body's immune system; this is I and this is not I. It wants to protect itself from others, to defend itself from insult or contradiction, and to appropriate all things for itself. It also gives the greatest collective sense of self that has been formed by its relatedness to all other sheaths of our being, and therefore can also be the core of selfishness.

Our ego in its selfness leads the soul activities to self needs and self gain. If the soul is body-bound, it follows that the ego will serve the soul in serving the past. All the capacities of soul look toward self-fulfillment and grati-fication through such egotism. However, the true I turns our service to the world. Instead of seeking justice for the self in the sentient soul, we seek justice for all. Instead of having understanding and compassion for our own plights in life, we have understanding and compassion for all.

Through our conscious striving for a relationship to the spirit, the human being gradually transitions from the ego's running our inner life toward the true I as the guide of our inner life. Rudolf Steiner stated that this guide is your one and only true guide. The true I orders the soul according to the laws of the spiritual community in brotherhood, equality, and freedom.

We are influenced by what we take in from the outer world through the sheath I, the ego. It is different with the true I, because we give to the world through the true I what is aligned to the spiritual life.

We pour all the influences that come to us from the outer world, which tear and distort us, back and forth into the sheath I; all the influences that go from one person to another in the characterized way impact the sheath I. The true, the actual I, which far exceeds the other, we must try to strengthen; then we will be invulnerable to the outer influences.[9]

Many know that this recognizing of the I as the true being is only the beginning of its journey, its initial birth. It will continue onward if or when the I is initiated and grows into the world of spirit; that is, initiated into a conscious relationship with the higher consciousnesses of the spiritual world. Then the true I is not only invulnerable to the outer influences it does not want to receive, it also holds the power to support others to find the higher in themselves.

The three realities of the human being—the body, soul, and spirit—are intimately connected with each other; they work upon each other, and are related. The outer bodies grow uniquely through the impressions given by the incarnating soul forces. These forces were developed in previous lives by the work of the I.

The soul is taken hold of and developed by the will of the individual. The soul is liberated by the I from its state of being body-bound, and is worked upon to strengthen and develop its capacities.

This results in the soul's capacity eventually to develop fully, and it allows the soul to receive insights from the spiritual world and be a bridge from the spirit toward the earthly world. Developing strength also allows the soul to withstand the influences of the outer world and from its outer conditioned self. Developing the ability to consciously receive insights that flow continuously from the spiritual world gives another level of strength and capacity to the soul. Then, being able to access the power to live these insights into the outer life develops yet another level of strength and capacity. The soul gains these capacities through the efforts of the individual will.

> The human being has to do consciously what the plant does unconsciously. Human beings as self-conscious beings and ego-bearers are required to bring about their development in themselves by their own efforts. At a certain stage they must be prepared to surrender whatever they have received from the outside and to give birth within their own ego, to their higher ego. Then the ego will not become hardened but will enter into a harmonious relationship with the entire world.[10]

The I awakens and is strengthened through the task of taking hold of the three soul forces, through discipline and determination to master and be responsible for the soul.

As Rumi beautifully puts it in the poem "Checkmate":

> A hide soaked in tanning liquor and becomes leather.
> If that tanner did not rub in the acid,
> the hide would get foul smelling and rotten.
> The soul is a newly skinned hide, bloody and gross.
> Work on it with manual discipline
> and the bitter tanning acid of grief,
> and you will become lovely and very strong.[11]

Once the I has developed certain capacities by taking hold of the soul in this way, once it has lit its lamp, it can be seen as ready for the journey of the spirit. The I can be initiated only by a spiritual activity higher than ourselves.

It is not easy to consider the idea of spiritual beings with a rational mind, and yet we can recognize that we have this eternal component in ourselves. Some know that if all else that is ourselves falls away and only this eternal part is left, we would simply be consciousness, beings of consciousness.

> I gaze into the darkness
> in it there arises a light—
> living light!
> Who is this light in the darkness?
> It is I myself in my reality.
> This reality of the I
> does not enter into my earthly life.
> I am but a picture of it
> but I shall find it again
> when with goodwill for the spirit
> I shall have passed through the gate of death.[12]

Steiner described the reality of consciousness that expresses in different degrees as "beings." "It is well never to lose sight of the fact that fundamentally all that exists in the universe is consciousness, consciousnesses. Anything outside the consciousness of beings of whatever order belongs to the realm of maya, the great illusion."[13]

Initiation into the reality of consciousnesses cannot be demanded, only prepared for; made ready for the journey that takes us beyond all life that is known up until now. The I is initiated by the higher beings, or the consciousnesses that extend beyond the individual power of illumination. These consciousnesses reside in and make up the spiritual world, and are also the true home of the I. The light is drawn by a greater light.

The soul can begin developing further only once the body is grown. The soul can be experiencing, gaining, and relating before the growth of the body is completed; but true soul development does not take place until adulthood, when the ego sheath has been born and can begin to consciously develop the soul. Every stage of human development is necessary; each step is surmounted before the next can unfold.

Rudolf Steiner spoke many times about the evolution of the collective consciousness of humanity. He pointed out that we have passed through the sentient soul age, a time when the instinctual mind was regarded as the most valuable; and after that we passed through the intellectual soul age, the Greco-Roman period, which lasted from 700 BC until the fifteenth century. For the last 600 years, and presently as a collective consciousness, we have entered the consciousness soul age. At each stage of consciousness the human being thinks, feels, and acts differently in the world.

A fourteenth-century person who spoke of the ideals of race, nation, and tribal membership would have been speaking in terms of the progressive tendencies of human evolution. Someone who speaks of the ideal of race, nation, and of tribal membership today is speaking out of the impulses that are part of the decline of humanity. Nothing is more designed to take humanity into its decline than the propagation of the ideals of the blood bond. Only the bonds of spiritual communion will bring a progressive element into the natural element of decline.[14]

As a collective consciousness, humanity as a whole has developed as far as the beginning of the consciousness soul age. This is why we see so many individuals awakening to their awareness of the greater life of spirit. Awakening not through religion or belief, but through the path of self-development (this does not exclude the possibility of awakening through religious worship). Every human being participating in life has the possibility to develop to the stage the collective consciousness has reached at that time in evolution. The progress of the human race toward freedom has already gone so far that it depends upon humanity itself whether we will sleep through this event or face it with fully wide-awake consciousness.[15]

In ancient India, when the word "self" was spoken, this never meant myself or the individual self, for this was never part of the consciousness at that stage. The self was the great self, the collective self, the spirit that they were not divided from. It was the task of the ancient Indian initiates to bring practices that would assist in the binding of the soul to the body to give the experience of the individualized self.

We needed to separate from the Godhead, as the spirit is called in the ancient text, to develop the free will to unite again with the godhead in full consciousness. The ancient yogic practices supported the binding of the soul to the body, bringing about in human evolution the capacity to develop the separated consciousness.

We can still use these practices today, but they work counter to the needs of today's consciousness. Our separated consciousness is now too strong. We have such a strong sense of self that we are unable to experience our connectedness to the whole. This may not be the case for every individual because the Earth is made up of human beings at varying stages of evolution. However, collective humanity is working at the evolutionary stage of releasing the soul from its body-dependent, separated existence, toward developing a rich inner life of liberated forces.

Many people practicing ancient meditative techniques, such as yoga, experience feeling connected, peaceful and centered. This is undoubtedly a true experience. We can even gain deep insights into the development of the bodily sheaths by binding the soul into the body in a less subjective way. The consciousness can experience the forces behind the physical sheaths, gaining insight into the past. This is a very different experience than holding the clarity of the awakened I in relationship to the living spiritual world in the present. Returning the consciousness to the body returns the consciousness to old states of awareness.

Powerful, calming, and centering, some of these ancient exercises relieve us of our personal struggles, yet keep us dependent on the body. The level now being asked of us is freedom from any transitory self, developing sense-free perception to live as soul in a non-sense perceptible world.

Many people are using ancient techniques such as mindfulness practices like watching the breath to manage the chaos of their speeding lives. This could be an indication of the collective weakness in the modern soul because, although this technique can bring calming and centering, it rarely brings soul strength or the tools required for our future stages of being. In the consciousness soul age we need our practice to directly strengthen the soul to meet the adversaries we are facing at this time. We need strength that can meet the inner and outer worlds; this is not the same task as it was thousands of years ago. Strength is needed to face what needs to be transformed now, both in ourselves and in the world around us.

Some of the old ways of being appeal to the human consciousness in our times; others, we are repelled by. We may look back to the thinking of the ancient Greco-Roman period. At that time some spoke of how the environment produced thoughts for them; that their thinking was not internalized, but externalized in the world around. Nowadays we see this as foolish and even ridicule it as religious conditioning, but the reality is that human consciousness was different in that epoch.

Our collective capacities are developing, and as humanity strives toward the future, new aspects of consciousness will be grasped, first by some and then by many, until they too become a part of the collective consciousness. The collective development allows all those who are living on earth to achieve it themselves, because the path has been made clear. Stages of development have been achieved by individuals striving on behalf of all. These stages that have been won by human efforts are also supported by the beings of progression, the spirits of light who change the ways they assist us according to our evolving needs. "In more recent times the spirits of light have changed their function; they now inspire human beings to develop independent ideas, feelings, and impulses for freedom; they now make it their concern to establish the bases in which people can be independent individuals."[16]

Where we are now, what we can achieve, we owe to those who have worked before us. Our capacity to develop the consciousness soul today is a result of many beings serving, striving, and sacrificing for the evolution of humanity. We are a part of this; and the more we achieve the more we must give back, if we are working out of the laws of the true I.

If our consciousness soul age continues to unfold and yet the ego continues to work for self and selfishness through its body-bound existence, then we will not see this stepping-stone possibility, which is the next step of working from the consciousness soul into the spiritual world and further developing our spiritual sheaths; rather, we will see all the devastating effects of the ego binding more strongly to the body. There is such a fine line between what is commonly known as the white path and the dark path. This fine line asks the question, is this for self or other? The consequences are not so fine.

In the case that human beings do not choose to develop a relationship to the spirit, but only to their separated selves, Steiner predicted that we will see all sorts of division, not only between countries and religions, but right down into families. We already see parents who do not connect to or understand their children, and children who cannot tolerate their parents. We see immense division between human beings, all working for themselves on behalf of their own self-needs. We are also seeing the unjust effects of some reaping benefits for themselves in ways that require them to actually harm others.

The consciousness soul is bound to the body, the physical sheath that separates me from the other. We will see greater conflict between individual beings unless at the same time we can liberate the soul from the body through the choice of the individual. "Since the fifteenth century, only since then has thinking been competent to bring the spiritual soul into the realm of the spirit, but at the same time also hinder it from entering the spiritual world."[17]

If we cannot liberate the soul from the body by the strength of the I, we will see all that gratifies the physical body gaining in importance and gaining higher and higher regard, and being presented as the only reality that exists. Already the sciences tell us there is no love, just hormones, such as dopamine and serotonin, and the chemistry of attraction, such as pheromones. More and more medical treatments will be developed to give so-called health to the body, while making the inner being sick. There will be nutritional plans given to develop clever people that advise exactly what nutrients to consume to develop greater brain function. Sex will be treated with greater separation from inner experience, and as a result all forms of sexual debauchery will arise. In this age the physical body will become god.

We have to tread this path and make our way through. It will be our own moral capacity that will prevent us from misusing the forces directed to the body in the consciousness soul age. Rudolf Steiner laid down the guideline in *Knowledge of the Higher Worlds:* for every step we take on the path of development, we should take three steps in our moral development, in perfecting ourselves toward the good. This holds true not only for those attempting to walk this path consciously, but for all humanity as it steps up to a new stage of awakening.

The heralding of the consciousness soul age requires greater capacity to work for the good of all and to see beyond our own needs, just as the divine-spiritual world does. Working tirelessly, regardless of which path we take, the spiritual world (or "the friend" as Rumi calls it) will continue to call us onward in our evolution.

> If you can't do this work yourself, don't worry
> you don't even have to make a decision,
> one way or another. The friend, who knows
> a lot more than you do, will bring difficulties
> as grief, and sickness, as medicine, as happiness...[18]

2

THE SOUL AND THE GROWTH
OF THE BODY

The meaning of life cannot have just one single answer, simply because in life we ourselves are not just one single self. The question of meaning arises from more than one aspect of our being. For the spirit, the meaning may be freedom. For the soul, the true meaning may be love. For the individual personality, the meaning may be the forming, pursuit, and realization of individual ideals. What we can be certain of is that these meanings awaken over time; and that they grow, develop, and expand throughout our lives.

How open we are to our growth and self-development comes not only from within us. Our readiness for this is laid also as foundations in our childhood. Whether we have the interest, the courage, and the openness to continue our growth in adulthood can be helped or hindered in our formative years. If we recognise that we have been hindered, on the one hand we will have a harder task in front of us, and yet by the fact that we choose to develop out of ourselves suggests that we must have brought with us the necessary interest, courage, and openness, since they were not provided by the important adults of our youth. When we have insight into what takes place in the world of the developing child, we can assess where we have come from, how we met our environment, and what indeed needs reshaping in our adulthood.

A majority of people in the world believe reincarnation to be true, yet it is not a common belief in the western worldview. There are some useful aspects to considering that there is only one life. Such a belief can help us make the best use of the life we have, rather than resign ourselves to karma, and such thoughts. However, in the heart of esoteric wisdom, evolution of consciousness can bear the necessary responsibility only if we consider that we played a part in the past, and will do so in the future. The soul of the past contributes to the present life, and what we gain in the present life will contribute to the next. In the growth of the vehicle of the body, the soul is contributing where it can to develop the necessary conditions for this incarnation.

The light you give off did not come from a pelvis.
Your features did not begin in semen.
— Rumi[19]

For approximately the first nineteen years of life the soul must concentrate its forces on the growth of the outer bodily vehicle in such a way that the body can allow further development of the soul in later life. What the soul gains as strength to hold the ground against the outer world, in the next life becomes the forming force that sculpts the physical body. The outer result of the incarnating soul's sculpting forces is expressed in the physical appearance. The stronger the force the soul bears with it into the world, the more individualized the outer body will appear, and therefore less influenced by the hereditary characteristics of the family. The inner expression of the strong soul is that the individual is less sculpted by the environment. The outer world wants to draw the soul into the laws of the earthly world, and bind it as a citizen of this world alone. The stronger the incarnating soul, the greater is its continual connection with its origin. It remains a connected citizen of the soul world, as well as participating as a citizen of the physical world.

Supporting Freedom in the Growing Child

All that is given out of anthroposophy is imbued with the spiritual wisdom of the human being's becoming. We can look at Waldorf education through this lens and see how it is steeped in esoteric knowledge. Steiner himself said "Waldorf education is the outcome of a total dedication to human freedom. It springs from the ideal to place human beings into the world in such a way that they can unfold their individual freedom."[20] We can all learn from what was given to the teachers, because what was given to the teachers was to advance the next stage of consciousness soul development.

The young child has been described as an imitator. We often think of this as one child copying the others, and the world around. The reality is that the soul of the young child continues to follow spiritual laws. In the spiritual world there is no division between self and the other; we live entirely in the outer world and the whole world is our inner being. All is within us. The young child learning to walk and speak does so from this same living within the other. The young child experiences the other from within its own being, within its own consciousness. This consciousness does not include an awareness of a freedom that gives the possibility to choose to switch imitation on or off, as is the possibility of the consciously developed adult.

As we work with the inner work path, certain exercises are given for us to regain this experience of living within the other. The living plant and dying plant exercise described in chapter 1 is one of them. When we penetrate such an important exercise, we begin to grow together with the outer world. We start to gain insight into the world of soul that the child is still open to. As adults, if we work with this exercise for some time, the experience grows and a kind of conscious soul-seeing emerges. Through such exercises we have a glimpse into what the child experiences, although for the child it occurs without training or wanting it. Blending into the world around happens to them; they are inwardly experiencing it. If we can grow sensitive to that truth, we are more able to care for the inner world of children and be more conscious of what we present for them to, as they do, drink in.

Children live unconsciously into the inner life of those in their presence. Therefore, Steiner indicated that it's not what you teach, but who you are that is the most important factor in supporting the growing child. He also suggests that if the child is having difficulties, the adults should first look within to see how they are being in the presence of the child. Up until the age of seven, the child needs to be surrounded as much as possible with love, joy, and warmth from adults. These feelings become a ground for continual soul growth in later life. The child who has been received in love grows into an adult who can give to the world, and at the same time be in a continual state of learning and developing from what the world can teach. If this ground is not supplied in childhood, then we see in the years from thirty-five to forty-two (which are a reflective seven-year cycle), adults who become closed and fixed in their character, and therefore stop learning from life.

In various lectures to teachers, Steiner called for reverence for the soul and spirit of the individual child. "The first prerequisite for a Waldorf teacher is to have reverence for the soul and spiritual potential that each child brings into the world."[21] He guided the teachers to teach in such a way that the child's soul could remain connected to the soul and spiritual worlds. This approach to teaching makes it possible for the sculpting forces that come toward the child from what is taught will not have an unhealthy effect upon the developing sheaths. These sculpting forces coming from the teaching will assist the incarnating soul in its forming of the bodily vehicle in which the soul will meet its destiny; the soul will not be hindered in this important task.

We do aim in full consciousness to aid and foster the healthy development of the child's physical body; for in this way the child's soul and spiritual nature is given

the best means of unfolding freely out of its own re-
sources. By damaging as little as possible the spiritual
forces working through the child, we give the child the
best possibility of developing healthily.[22]

What are these damaging sculpting forces that can
affect the developing child? It is what lives in us that
keeps us separated from the whole. Our own personal
sympathies and antipathies limit our openness to the
child. There are many things in our own nature that make
us unfree, although we may be unaware of this lack of
freedom because we are bound to these preferences.
Although we may want the best for the developing child,
we do not realize the consequences of forcing ourselves
on this developing being. We want the child to be this or
that because we ourselves admire this or that; or because
we will be seen in a better light if the child becomes this
or that.

This imposition of sculpting forces has happened in our
own development. Think of your youngest years. This is
a time when children should be held in the world in such
a way that they can experience that the world is good.
Instead of that, we are often given instructions about how
we should be good. What did you need to do to be good
as a child? Be useful to others, be quiet? Be sweet and
kind, be mother's helper, be father's strong boy, be indus-
trious? Be clean and tidy, be well mannered, be cute, and
so forth? You may notice if you remember the "good"
that you were supposed to be, that these requirements still
could be an unconscious motivator in your life even now.

We can also see the residue of our earlier conditioning when we consider that the child needs to know the
world is beautiful. Instead children are given all the
conditions of right and wrong according to the culture
and the community. If we remember what was asked of
us, to be beautiful or attractive to our family group, we
may be surprised at how this still influences us. What
were the attractive qualities that would make you part
of the group? Did you need to be independent, be physically attractive, be smart? Be confident, be forthright, be
mild and yielding? Be intelligent, be funny, and so forth?
These requirements may feel so much a part of you that
it's hard to separate yourself from this conditioned lack
of freedom.

We do not see the negative consequences of stuffing
children with our own opinions and preferences. Steiner
said that if we could see what impact we are having, we
would work entirely differently to support children's freedom. We would see that "what is stuffed into the child in
that way will work out karmically to make the grown
man or woman a hard, dry nature, prematurely old,
because the very core of being is killed."[23] Strong souls
bring the strength with them that can resist the sculpting
forces of the other, of the outer world.

The incarnating soul not only sculpts the physical
body, setting the ground for its ongoing development, but
it also must relate what comes from the outer world to
the inner world. The young child still participating in the
soul-spiritual world carries its laws into the earthly life.
The rhythms of the soul-spiritual world have an effect

on the healthy rhythms of the physical body. Earthly rhythms, when separated from the connection with the higher worlds, can have an unhealthy effect on the physical sheaths. Every disconnected rhythm has to be assimilated by the human being; must be rhythmatized inwardly to overcome these foreign effects. The strong soul can assimilate the patterns of the external world and overcome their negative effect. For instance, take the effects of technology. As we sit in front of the computer we become aware that our thinking rhythm and our nervous system are changed into a different and faster pattern. The pace of external life often runs at a different pace than the rhythms of a harmonious inner life.

To understand children's ability to experience what sounds toward them out of things, we can also develop the capacity to hear as they hear. In *Knowledge of the Higher Worlds,* Steiner presented one of the listening exercises.[24] He asked us to direct our attention to the outer world of sounds, and try to notice the difference between sounds that arise from inanimate objects and the sounds arising from living beings. Walk outside and direct your attention to the bird sounds, then to the traffic sounds; move attention between the two, focusing so much attention on each sound that you can block out the effects of all others. Or compare a bell sound or an object banging, with the sound of a human speaking. We begin to awaken to the fact that when human beings communicate they also communicate something other than words; they communicate the soul world of their inner experience. All living beings communicate their inner experience; the pleasure, the pain. As we learn to listen, we can hear even the source of the thought; was it egotistical or genuine? Was what was spoken borrowed knowledge, or the other's own experienced knowledge?

Everything external possesses a form, and also a rhythm, which is an activity or motion that takes effect in the inner responses. When we look at a plant that is living and growing, we perceive it with our senses; but we also experience it inwardly. When we compare this with the plant that is dying and decaying, we can experience inwardly a very different activity, movement, or rhythm. When we give our attention to a computer screen or a television screen, we inwardly experience the rhythm of glass, plastic, metal, in addition to the stimulation of the information in the intellect.

For the human soul that recognizes the connection, a meeting point, there is a big difference between what lives in itself and what lives in the outer world. The soul recognizes the living, growing, flourishing that exists in its own nature; and the dying decaying that exists in its own being. The soul perceives a truth in the world of nature, and the relationship of that truth to its own inner world. The soul perceives the wisdom-filled harmony between itself and the outer world. It experiences a belonging, a connectedness, and a continuum between self and other. On the other hand, the soul cannot find in the same way on the screen and with plastic what it experiences within its own being. These feel unrelated, disconnected, void, and empty in comparison to the living relationship with the natural world.

When the child sees an animal on a screen, the inner experience is screen, plastic, and information. The child tries to relate what it already knows to what it sees and what is now being told and shown. The young child may cry because on the screen it sees the baby chicken being killed by a fox. The child cries because that loss and that pain is all it can relate to internally in its own world of experience. Then the child is told, "This is nature; you do not need to cry." Internally the child probably will build an antipathy for the fox that can hurt and cause pain. This has absolutely nothing to do with the fox or the essence of fox-ness. The screen child does not learn about the fox as true knowledge; but only as the information the child is given, and its own inner relating to what it sees, including the effects of the background music, screen experiences, and so forth.

Then a studio makes an animation film of a fox. Now the fox is a lovable character that is trying to help the poor and win the princess's hand in marriage by showing its skills and its achievements. Now what does the young child do with this new picture of the fox? The child has to separate what it has learned from the fox that ripped the chicken's head off, causing inner upset, from what it has learned from the fox whose antics are now so amusing. The child cannot unite these pictures inwardly because they do not belong together. The child's inner life begins to split and have separate compartments of liking and not liking; good and bad; things I want to see (the animated fox), and things I don't want to see (a real fox). This has nothing to do with the fox; only with the dividing nature

43

of the materialistic world and the power it has to separate us from our connection to the whole.

When the child sees a fox in life, the child's inner experience is the power of the living creature, the unique quality of the animal; and that resounds as an inner quality, perhaps not even a describable quality. But the child recognizes the relatedness between itself and the other. The child experiences that what lives out there lives also in the inner soul capacities, but in a human way. The experience of the inner rhythms that the fox invokes is not alien to the child; the child looks on in wonder. The experience of the living animal brings an inner activity that leads to knowledge, not information. The child develops knowledge of the qualities of each living creature; knowledge of the place each has in the whole and our relatedness to it.

Although deeper learning is no different for adults, children live in the place of inner susceptibility, which means they are more directly, deeply, and therefore more easily affected by the world around them. They live in wonder, which is the open doorway. As adults, we have to adjust inwardly to experience the effects of the outer world as an inner activity. For example, for us as adults to do the plant exercise or the sound exercise that was mentioned, we need to make some inner adjustments. We pass living and dying aspects of nature regularly, and we hear sounds all the time; but we do not recognize their effect on us. We need first to make time to observe what takes place inwardly, looking at the living, flourishing plant, and holding an awareness of the inner activity that it invokes; then looking at the dying and decaying plant, and keeping an eye on the changing that streams inwardly. Through the growing plant we inwardly can experience something like an expansion of activity; with the dying plant we inwardly experience something like contraction of the inner streaming. When we hear people talking from their egotistical gratification of themselves or talking with honest inner striving, we experience different inner activities. This contrast educates us to the nature of these processes in the soul world.

When we try to assess how to approach these exercises in a productive way, we recognize that we need to give time to allow the perceptions and experiences to meet in us. Also we need to adjust our inner pace, and we have to center ourselves. We cannot do these exercises from the periphery of our intellect. Most children are highly suscep-tible to the effects of outer impressions up until around the eleventh year, when there is a neurological housecleaning. Then, the parts of the brain and nervous system that have not been used actively begin to be pared back, while the neurological pathways that have been trodden frequently become strengthened. This is one main reason why, when we learn another language after the age of eleven, we more often hold the accent of our native tongue.

These years of childhood are a time when children are molded by many things; some that are true, some that are useful, and some that are errors. The young child is also molded by the community rules. These rules are taken on as unconscious beliefs by the developing child. Through the sphere of the etheric body, the body of life, the child becomes a citizen not only of the earthly world, but also of a particular community, family, race, or religion. These beliefs act to integrate the child into a given society. Some of these laws or rules may emulate the laws of the spiritual life; others may be disconnected laws and rules that are human-made conditions, often merely serving those who enforce them. The laws also can be a reflection of the consciousness to which humanity has been able to develop at that time. We may notice that all human-made conditions change in time—in the direction of the truth of spiritual life, we hope.

For example, it is a law in the spiritual world that the capacities of the individual soul determine the tasks it carries. However, in human-made laws, up until recently it has been your gender, whether you are born man or woman, that determines the task you may carry in life.

Sometimes these rules are widespread. For example, in the past if you were born in a male body you would protect and provide for the females in the society. This used to be a conditioning. Sometimes these rules are more particular to certain cultures: Polynesian men may wear skirts; in general, western men may not. It has been recently, only in the last 200 years, that women in the western world may wear trousers. Cultural practices change over time, and when we look back on the ones that have changed, they often seem childlike to the modern consciousness. In the next 200 years we will look back on the question of who can marry whom, and we will consider the childishness of the cultural practices of these times. As the human being awakens to the reality of the soul-spiritual nature that lives beyond gender with its emphasis on the outer body, then the question of whom I partner with will be a soul-spiritual question.

In the age of the consciousness soul, many young people do not want to be confined to the conditions of the past, to old cultural forms. They are coming with a new way of looking at the world, and they can feel extraordinarily isolated when the old forms are forced upon them. We need far more awareness, especially as educators of these consciousness soul-era children. How easy is it for a teacher to say, "I need all the boys to move the tables and chairs, and the girls to go and pick flowers and arrange them beautifully in the class." More often, if teachers would only stop and think about what they are saying, they would recognize that it is not even their own beliefs, but their parent's conditioning speaking to this future humanity. So many young people are ready to be acknowledged and given tasks not according to their gender but according to their capacities and interests.

We see the emphasis on gender conditioning particularly highlighted in the instance of rites of passage into manhood and womanhood. Usually the girls are guided to join in a circle talking about menstruation and body image, whereas the boys are taken into physical challenges and to test themselves against the elements. These ancient initiation rites were developed and essential at a time when human evolution and consciousness needed such differentiations because of the need to individualize in the outer body. The oldest cultures of the world continue to honor their forefathers and foremothers with the rites and rituals of their tasks.

For a long time, effects of this continued to resound in the human psyche. These practices became rites of passage in which the development of the body and its capacity to procreate were central to the individual's becoming a full member of the community. Sexual maturity was the gauge for adulthood up until the dawn of the consciousness soul era when a new awareness of self emerged.

Now every woman knows she did not become a woman simply because she could menstruate. And every young girl knows that this biological process has little to do with her own individual capacity. She didn't create the blood or sweep the ovum down the fallopian tube; and yet this is being celebrated and marked as such an important achievement, and measure of who she is. The focus on the sex of the child and the social gender conditions amplify this one-sided sexualization of the human body. In our times this has devastating consequences, such as the over-sexualization of young people. I have had many conversations with young people who refuse to enter into these practices, or feel diminished by them. The generation now arising needs a new rite to recognize achieving adulthood.

We do need to find a way forward, but not by emphasizing the physical vehicle. To have a true understanding of being born "man" or "woman" (what Steiner called our area of least freedom), we need to separate conditioning given by social preferences from genuine soul experiences. Soul experiences may be gained differently in one vehicle or another, and stand behind the reason that we usually alternate male and female incarnations.

Things are rapidly changing in this area. Many of the women I work with are not mothers; they are not intending to be a mother or are biologically unable to be a mother, but they feel diminished by society for not using their reproductive organs. Many men who separate from their partners, do not understand why they cannot have equal custody and care of their children. These old forms around gender inequality are not useful for the future of the consciousness soul era. If the future of the human being will be a greater conscious relationship to the Spirit, then it is from this place that we should ask questions of how to move forward, rather than repeat the ancient past.

When a musician plays a wonderful piece of music, the instrument is not placed on stage and applauded. We applaud the musician's capacity to play the instrument. As the era of soul-spiritual awareness unfolds, we will more and more recognize the human body as the instrument, as the vehicle.

Recently while attending a genetics conference, I brought up the subject of the soul to a group of young geneticists. Some were dismissive of the idea that there could be anything other than the physical body. For others it was different; they used the analogy that the body is a vehicle and the soul drives the vehicle. They said that "Everyone wants to drive a Mercedes." My reply was, "Is this true? What if you're going to travel Route 66 in the States? Would you really want a Mercedes for that? Or going into the bush in outback Australia, would you really want a Mercedes then?" We always need to be aware that the vehicle is part of the soul's creating; it is not a random vehicle. Every feature changes how you meet the world, and how the world meets you.

Imagine for a moment traveling Route 66 in a Mercedes; and then traveling Route 66 in a Corvette. It's not just getting from A to B, but also what is drawn toward you while you are traveling there. The type of vehicle contributes and makes a difference to the encounters on the journey. Encounters that are necessary for ongoing development.

Genetics has now developed to the point where we can give a profile of the fetus's DNA from the maternal blood at only ten weeks' gestation. If we believe we all want to drive Mercedes, then we will more readily interfere with any vehicle that does not have this "Mercedes" quality. Even the strong soul may not be able to withstand this kind of interference with the bodily sheaths.

> The more this emerges in individual people, not merely as a theory but as a feeling, a feeling of dependence on a purely earthly inherited characteristic, the more oppressive and dreadful will it gradually become. And this feeling will increase in strength very rapidly in the decades ahead; it will intensify to a point of becoming unbearable, for it is connected with another feeling—a certain feeling of the worthlessness of human existence.[25]

Especially between the years of seven and fourteen, the child needs adults and teachers who can be authorities worthy of trust, as well as a source of truth. If this is provided to the child, this trust becomes initiative and courage in the adult soul. This kind of authority worthy of trust and truth is not an intellectual concept based on what the teacher tells the child. It is the consciousness behind what is spoken that the child meets. The child experiences an inwardly stressed teacher as one who is speaking words that are coupled with the place of stress the teacher speaks from. An untruth is words spoken coupled with the consciousness of deception. Children know the source of the teacher's words because they can hear it. If this ground was not given in childhood, initiative and courage diminish in the young adult in the years from age twenty-eight to thirty-five, a period that reflects the earlier years.

At around the fourteenth year the child is what Steiner called "earth ripe." The soul has now fully descended from the pre-birth existence and stands meeting the world that is before it. "Subconsciously or semi-consciously it makes adolescents compare the world they have now entered with the world that they formerly had within themselves. This in turn gives rise to the tumultuous relationship between the adolescent and the surrounding world, lasting from the fourteenth year to the twenties."[26] The soul has been sculpting the body and bringing its relationship between the inner and outer worlds into rhythm; now it must encounter the world fully.

It is the strength of the soul that allows it to bring its own sculpting forces to withstand the forces streaming toward it from the outer world of separation and division. It is the capacity of the soul to stay connected to the spiritual laws that allow it to withstand conditioning that attempts to indoctrinate it entirely into the collective social laws. It is the soul's capacity to live what it has brought from the Spirit into the world that enables it to withstand the onslaught of earthly errors that now surround it.

This is the most challenging time for adolescents. They are meeting the world that has removed itself from the spirit, knowing they have to participate in redirecting the world toward the spirit once again. Young people at this time do not need the authority of a teacher; they do, however, need to encounter adults who have found their place, or their task, in redirecting the world toward the spiritual.

To enter into understanding adolescent experience, we can work with another important inner work exercise. In this exercise we direct our attention to the wishes and desires living in other human beings. We try to recall a time when we saw a person immersed in a desire for something. We build the picture inwardly as clearly as possible and surrender ourselves to the picture in complete dedication to the memory. Now we pay close attention to the feelings that are awakened by the image we have formed. As far as possible, we allow our inner life to become united with the inner activity of the one who desires. The second part of this exercise is now to recall someone whose desire was fulfilled, again building a vivid mental picture of the outer circumstances, at the same time focusing on the inner experience that fulfilling the desire evoked in the other, and now in yourself. If we practice this sincerely, in time we become awake to the astral world that sweeps through adolescent souls without their capacity to control it.

This inner schooling exercise allows us to recognize the inner world of adolescents. They now stand in the earthly life as we do, but they have another sensitivity to the soul world of all the others around them. They are particularly affected by the desire body of those they come into contact with. The term "friendfluence" has arisen out of several studies that show how our friends influence us in both positive and negative ways. If your friends smoke, you are forty-five percent more likely to be a smoker; if they are obese you are forty-five percent more likely to be overweight yourself. We can understand these studies in the light of the astral body of the teenager, which extends into others' desires, so that they become as though their own. The fact that this continues into adulthood may say something about weakness in our inner capacities.

In adolescents, the division between others inner life and their own inner life is blurred, particularly now in the realm of longings and desires. They feel compelled to fulfill the desires arising within them, even when the desire did not originate within them. This can lead adolescents toward many distractions and diversions in these years, even to the point of destruction of themselves and others, if they submerge into the desire bodies of others intent on destruction. Adolescents can be supported in this struggle by adults around them who have transformed their personal desire into love for their tasks in the world.

Adolescents need teachers who love their task. In the reflective seven years from twenty-one to twenty-eight, young adults who have been supported in the right way in adolescence will have true interest in the world. If they were unsupported in this way, then in the reflective age from twenty-one to twenty-eight, we will not see this interest in the world, only interest in self-gratification.

What lives in the adults, the parents, the educators, and the community can have a deep effect on the developing sheaths, if the incarnating soul does not have the capacity to withstand these outer influences. We do not, however, have any ability to affect the soul capacities that the children bring with them, only the sheaths into which they incarnate. We cannot grow another being's soul capacities. This is entirely in the individual's hands; but we can set the ground to not impinge upon their inborn freedom. We can set the ground that makes it more possible for the individual ego to develop the soul for itself in adulthood.

As parents or educators of children, our primary influence affects the development of the three bodily sheaths. We may not recognize this because we think we are educating the soul of the child. However these outer sheaths, those of the body, play the most important role in how the soul is able to enter into the world.

To understand this relationship, imagine a mirror; imagine that the physical body is the glass of the mirror, and the etheric body is the silver paint that allows for reflection of the image. Then the astral body is the light needed so that the mirror can reflect the image of the human soul. The ego perceives the image that is reflected.

If the glass is cracked, there will be tremendous error in how the human being can see itself; the image will be distorted, depending on the nature of the crack. If the glass is broken, the image is more or less distorted; distorted from the whole true image. If the paint is chipped off, there will be gaps in the image that will prevent us from experiencing the whole as it is in reality. If the light is too dim we will not see the details of the image.

The soul requires a healthy vehicle to have a true and healthy reflection of itself. In this way we can begin to understand the principle that is laid down in anthroposophic medicine that says all mental illness has a physical cause. If you are looking into a cracked and chipped mirror, it makes you appear as though one eye were missing or distorted. The features are all in the wrong place; if this was your reality, you would see the world differently. You would respond to things that others do not see. The soul itself is not so out of balance, but how it is able to perceive itself in the mirror of the body may be very out of balance.

The ego may perceive the image as self, but the image is not the self. The I can know only from within that the soul is independent from the mirror. "We do not see ourselves aright if we say 'Here I am, this robust real person standing upon the earth, here I am with my innermost being.' We see ourselves aright only if we say our true being is in the spiritual world; and what is here of us on earth is but a picture and image of our true being."[27]

It is first the individual soul that creates this mirror in the right way for its needs in life. Then, wherever the incarnating soul is unable to carve and paint and illuminate out of itself, it is open to the hands of others: the parents, teachers, and community. Steiner expressed this to the teachers: "Even if we, the educators, wanted it, we have no influence over the development of what belongs to the realm of soul and spirit. All one can do is to help toward a free use of physical capacities by means of the soul and spirit." [28]

We can recognize the capacities individuals bring with them, either as gifts or as tasks to work on, and we can support and guide them in their task. There are the three soul capacities that need to be worked on by the ego, and at times we can see a clear dominance of one of these soul processes. The sentient soul-dominant child has different struggles from those of the intellectual soul-dominant child and the consciousness soul-dominant child. We all have all three soul activities, yet one may be dominating at different stages of the individual child's development; and we can guide children through this.

Currently there is a rapidly increasing trend in diagnosing children with learning difficulties at home and school, and also the recognition that children are struggling to live harmoniously within themselves and in their relationship to the world. This has resulted in the extraordinary increase of childhood learning disorders and labels. Being able to distinguish between learning difficulties that arise out of imbalances in the bodily sheaths (which affect the soul's connection and harmonious reflection) and the imbalances that arise out of the dominance of one of the three soul activities is essential in supporting the child in a correct way.

The child whose physical sheaths have been disturbed requires physical support, which can take the form of interventions such as changing sensory input into the child's world, changing nutrition, and giving anthroposophic therapies and treatments. However, if the difficulty is arising from the dominance of one of the soul sheaths, then the teacher and parents can guide and support the child in such a way that the soul dominance does not prevent learning.

We have many ways of assessing the vehicle that the soul will use as its instrument, and these have been written about it in other anthroposophic works. We look toward the constitutional nerve-sense system or metabolic system dominance from birth onward, which may be indicated in one way by a child having a small or large head. Then from age seven onward, the temperaments are assessed; and beginning in the teenage years we see the importance of the planetary characteristics, which reveal the final stamp of the vehicle that the soul will live into.

Presented here are three brief descriptions of how soul dominance may show itself in the child in the classroom. However each should be adapted to the developmental tendencies for the particular age of the child. The constitution (founded on the physical body), the temperament (founded on the etheric body) and the planetary characteristics (founded on the astral body) will also affect how soul dominance will present, but the essential quality outlined here will still show itself through these outer sheaths.

Sentient soul-dominant children seem to go to school in order to have fun. They often move in groups, and seem to knit and bind to the class community. They like doing things with the whole class. They are often passionate and full of life, as well as reactive and intense. They can have difficulty following the rules of the class and rules of games, the laws of math, and so forth. These children often struggle with learning difficulties until the rules and laws finally sink in. They can be very reactive emotionally, and wild in their outbursts. When they have a tantrum they do not know what they are doing; it's intense and uncalculated. When they want something, they will use whining, fighting, or demanding behavior to wear the adults down in order to get what they desire. It's hard to reason with them, but they can be distracted from the emotional intensity, especially with humor. They feel things very intensely when they think they are missing out on something, or when they don't get what they want. For them it is a soul longing that remains unfulfilled and burns within; they may try many ways to get what they are longing for, including unmanageable or defiant behaviors.

Sentient soul dominant-children need to be supported to learn the rules and the laws of the home and the classroom (of course these must be thought through in relationship to the well-being of the age and the needs of the child). Support comes not from intellectually telling them over and over what the rules are, but by guiding them physically along with songs and, importantly, with rhythms that become healthy conditions that begin to live in them. They learn well, especially when the whole class is taught the lesson together. They rebel if they think a rule is being placed only upon them.

One of the worst things we can do for these children is to allow them to get what they want by using the force of their emotions. If the parent or educator has recognized that what the child wants is not appropriate, or not what the child needs, the adult must hold the healthy boundaries for the child. This means the adult must stand in love and warmth, guiding the child out of love for the child's becoming, and wanting the child to become all it is able to be. If the child wears us down through constant nagging or annoying behaviors, and we end up giving into them for our own peace, this is detrimental for the well-being of the child.

Intellectual soul-dominant children attend school to learn. They often don't want to miss school, because they might miss something important. They feel they need to know everything in order to be right, or get it right. They easily learn the rules of the class, and can even act as the class police, telling the teacher when other children are not following the rules properly. They can learn abstractly at an early age. They pick up intellectual thinking and learning; but they often suffer from anxiety because of this intellectual prematurity, and the pressure of getting it right. After an emotional outburst, these children might apologize, and even set their own punishment.

They are able to make friends easily, but orient to like-minded others. In this way they can form and control who's in and who's out of the groups at school. They like working in a small group rather than with the whole class because they don't accept all the members of their class, and they wish to join with those who are more like themselves. They have a strong fear of rejection and a need for acceptance; this can be the reason for good behavior. But in teenage years it can also be the reason they follow their peers into destructive behavior.

Unfortunately, these children are often praised for their anxious participation in school. Because the mass consciousness still lives in the intellectual soul age and bases authority on who knows the most or who has the most credentials to their name, we tend to favor the intellect. Cramming these children with intellectual ideas is detrimental for them. But because they appear to manage, we fail to account for their needs, even though the anxiety levels in school children are growing at a rapid pace.

It is not just the effects on the human soul that we are concerned about, however. Because of the intimate relationship between the developing soul and the bodily sheaths, this intellectual education also works upon the future physical health. In *The Kingdom of Childhood* Steiner gave some specific effects for the seven- to twelve-year-old. "If you fill children with all kinds of intellectual teaching during this age (and this will be the case if we do not transform into pictures everything that we teach), then later they will suffer the effects in their blood vessels and in their circulation.... The effects on the child's soul take effect in the body, as they act as a unity."[29] These children are seen as the good learners, the good students in the class, and overlooked in their need for support. They are rarely sent for extra learning support, even though there is clearly stress in their system.

Academic, intellectual learning has taken hold of many schools, threatening even the Waldorf schools. Instead of ushering in the new age that will support the souls that are incarnating into the consciousness soul times, schools are bowing to the pressures from parents and the governing boards without placing the child's future at the center of the teaching.

What these children need is to be guided to seek not just information, but true knowledge, which can come only from their individual relationship to a subject. They need to be supported to find their individual passions, what really speaks to them and the capacities that they have brought with them. They need support to stand as being different from the group, and encouraged to be unique. They can be helped by not allowing them to have only one defined group of friends throughout the school year, but by having them work with others in the class who are not like themselves.

Consciousness soul-dominant children seem to be at school in order to teach others, or perhaps even to experiment on others, especially when they are not being met adequately by the education or the adults around them. For example, when a teacher is stressed, she may pick up her favorite cup, make a cup of tea, and sit in her comfortable chair away from the children, trying to give herself some "me time." Consciousness soul children seem more calculated when throwing a tantrum. They don't break just anything randomly they can put their hands on; they choose the teacher's favorite cup, and break that. Whenever we reflect on their actions, and see not just the meanness, we recognize that they were telling us something; something that we were not looking at.

They may put up a hand and ask the teacher, "Why don't you like this subject?" They are often seen as unique characters, even a bit quirky; or as strong individuals. In a group, they stand out. They tend not to have closely bonded friendships outwardly, especially not group-bonded friendships. They orbit like distant planets on the outside of the groups in the class; and may touch in to all of the groups at some point. They do not knit or bind in the collective consciousness or experience of the class. Yet they feel they belong to their class. They often prefer to work alone, and to be individually disciplined and instructed.

Because of their calculated behavior, which sometimes comes across as experimenting with others' feelings or experimenting with boundaries, and even being manipulative, we can recognize their need to learn reverence. They need to be supported in finding ways to come to reverence as they are growing.

These children can appear to have learning difficulties because they cannot learn abstractly; and they seem difficult in class because they accept only the rules they believe are right. They experience a lot of isolation, some may manage this, but if they are supported as individuals they can even stand strong in this isolation. If the school is focused primarily on intellectual soul students, consciousness soul children may feel that they are wasting time being at school.

Consciousness soul-dominant children can be misdiagnosed with learning disorders, such as being diagnosed on the Autism or Asperger's spectrum. Sentient soul children are more often given ADHD labels or oppositional defiance disorder labels. This is most likely to happen in a school where the old intellectual soul era is being crammed into the children. This practice is going against what all of the children are bringing in the consciousness soul era, regardless of individual soul dominance. Both the sentient soul-dominant child and the consciousness soul-dominant child can have great difficulties in school because of the school's limitations. They may even act up in similar ways, but it always comes from a different place. There is a presence that the consciousness soul-dominant children carry. They know what they are doing. The sentient soul-dominant child is lost in the experience of the doing. Something has a grasp on them, and they can't stop themselves. With the rapid rise of childhood disorder labels, we need to consider that the children may be healthy, and the education may be unhealthy. "Education and training take on a completely new significance in our modern time; and in fact there should be no more teaching without insight into the relation of the human being to the spiritual world.... That is the battle arising."[30]

What can we bring that is supportive, not only in childhood, but that continues to be the foundation that the children when grown into adults will stand upon as they attempt to work with self-development of the soul? We recognize that Steiner instructed the early Waldorf teachers to work out of the era of the consciousness soul, to support the next step of development in humanity. They were given definite requirements, not just suggestions. What was asked of the teachers? There are three primary areas that the teachers were instructed to focus on, which reveal the needs of our times.

The following is a collection of these points, divided here into three areas.

How We Teach: Love

These teachers were asked never to teach abstractly to the young child, but to keep each concept and lesson connected to the whole. While teaching a part, the teacher would need to inwardly hold the connection of each part as it is united to a whole. Teachers were asked to hold inner pictures of what they are teaching. They were asked to bring life to all that is given to the children as education; to express everything external (such as a mountain) not as a dead piece of matter, but as a living being.

In short, the teachers were asked to love what they taught. Genuine love for another is never based on having sympathy for particular characteristics of the one that is loved. Such sympathy arises when I feel pleased by those characteristics; they satisfy me. This is more a love for my own experience, not a giving to the other. The Love that is spoken of here means uniting ourselves with the subject we need to teach. It means deeply involving our inner life with the subject matter. The content becomes alive in us, and we grow from taking it in. Even if the teacher has taught the same subject many times, with each meeting something new is awakened. If the teachers love what they are teaching, the children will love what is taught. The teachers, in fact, do exactly what they want the children to do, and that is to unite themselves with the content of the teaching, not just learn information. The child as an imitator will do what the teacher does with the lesson. If the teacher's inner life is united with what is taught, if he or she is living in the inner pictures, then the child will follow this because the child lives where the teacher lives.

How We Stand in Ourselves: Freedom

The teachers were asked to leave their workaday, everyday selves, outside the classroom. They need to make the effort to bring with them what the children need. The kindergarten teachers need to bring love, warmth, and joy with them into the class to surround the children. Such a consciously created environment would result in the children's eventually growing into adults who are open to learning and giving of themselves to the world. Without these qualities entering somehow into the young child's world, the child could become an adult with a closed, fixed personality, unable to continue growing. The class teachers need to show authority that is worthy of trust, and to be a source of truth. Such teaching will result in the children's growing into adults who have courage and initiative in their lives. Without these qualities guiding the child in its life, the eventual adult would be slothful, lazy, and uninspired. The teachers of adolescents need to have deep interest in what they teach. This interest results in eventual adults who have true interest in the world. Without the teacher's love of the task being seen and experienced by the adolescents, when they are adults they would be interested only in themselves.

Facing such high ideals, before we adults give up on the responsibility of educating the next generation, we can take solace in these words from Rudolf Steiner as he lets us know the children can still transform themselves as adults:

> If education has not helped them in this way, they will find it difficult to work on their character, and they will have to resort to the strongest measures; they will need to devote themselves to deep meditative contemplation of certain qualities and feelings in order to impress these consciously on their soul....
>
> ... Through the play of the ego we can remold our character in later life."[31]

HOW WE WORK WITH THE SPIRIT: REVERENCE

Reverence is the key in all matters of being with children; this means reverence for the wisdom of the spiritual world that is working with the children, as well as the individual soul-spiritual capacities they bring with them. We need to guide them as best we can from the wisdom of the evolving consciousness given out of spiritual science.

Steiner encouraged the early Waldorf teachers to work directly with their individual relationship to the spiritual world. He gave them exercises to do before entering into sleep, such as reviewing the day spent with the class; contemplating the needs of the children; talking with a child's guiding spirit beings when seeking insight into how to support a particular child. These are all indicators of this spiritual work. Teachers were also guided to work together, such as with the child study or the inner work given directly to them, known as the college imagination.

Paramount in developing reverence is working with the spiritual world, or with the idea of other consciousnesses that are beyond our own.

Everything that was asked of the Waldorf teachers was intended to work out of the striving of the teacher's ego in transforming the consciousness soul. This is the place where we all need to be working as adults if we are to serve the future development of humanity. We work into the world out of reverence, love, and freedom. In the age of the consciousness soul, more than ever, we need to be strong souls capable of meeting what the world of materialism is becoming, and to transform it.

> Out of the gravity of the times
> must be born the courage to act.
> Give to teaching what the spirit gives you,
> and you will free humankind
> from the crushing mountain of materialism
> bearing down on it.[32]

If children's growth has gone well, as adults their souls will be ready and prepared to take on further development. They will be interested in the world, have courage and initiative, and be in a state of continual learning, while giving of themselves to the world around. These capacities put the individual in a good place to begin the necessary work of self-development. This leads to the three soul sheaths being capable of receiving from the spiritual world, and capable of giving what is received into daily life.

3

The I and the Development
of the Soul

The work of developing the self is the work of developing inner capacities and liberating the soul from patterns of being. The liberated soul can receive higher spiritual insights, with the aim of living these insights in order to care for the world around us. Self-development can take many forms. It can involve a defined meditative practice, as outlined in *The Inner Work Path: a Foundation for Meditative Practice,* and it can be taken hold of in everyday life experiences.

There are two primary possibilities for the soul to develop: consciously, by the efforts of the individual working on the soul directly, or by the efforts of the higher I working through the world and on the soul indirectly through the creation of external circumstances. Usually both are happening simultaneously.

In our time it is perfectly possible through inner self-disciplining and training of the will, to take in hand one's development, which is otherwise left to education and the experiences of life. Then without ascetic practices, one loosens the soul-spiritual from the bodily nature. The first discovery when such training of the will is undertaken for the sake of self-improvement is that a continuous effort is needed.[33]

Invariably, everyone needs to work on all three soul sheaths. We should not see this as a problem of short-comings; rather, it is an opportunity that will strengthen the individual. It is also important to recognize that it is in our task, in our love for our work, our earthly task, that we are more capable of taking up this great work of self-development because we do so for others.

We do not need to have accomplished this work of self-development before working in the world; rather, we can use the opportunity of our world work to fuel our development. If we all waited to be perfect at our given task before we took a role in life, there would be no one performing their duties. The soul is here to develop; and through our relationship to the world, we can accomplish that. When you have completely learned all that you can learn in your task, you would need to change your work. Once you have perfected something you are moved on to a greater challenge. When there is nothing left for you to learn in this life you are moved on.

Everyone has gifts, and in the giving out of these capacities the inner being develops further. If we are fortunate, our work is our task and therefore is the very place where we can give and receive at the same time.

We see people in numerous positions of work; some are in their task, and no matter what the position, they are shining in it. It is the ground of both their giving and receiving. Sometimes you meet those who are in a position only because they have been conditioned to enter that work by family, by finances, or by social standing. These people appear out of place in the task. What they receive is mostly material, and therefore not nourishing to their inner being. They spend their time trying to find other ways to gain inner nourishment.

I once heard an anthropologist speaking about the love of his work. He said, "I have never had a job in my life; I have always had my work." The word "job" comes from a French word that means "to devour." The word "work" is derived from a Greek word meaning "to alight, to inspire, to create." No matter what you do, if it is your work it will be a part of the path of development. If it is a job, you may need to look elsewhere to cultivate the conditions under which development can unfold.

For the soul to develop to its potential, the ego must take hold of the soul capacities, liberate them from their body-bound activity that binds them to the past, and strengthen them independently from the body. The ego gains ever more strength by overcoming certain soul tendencies and cultivating others. It is not asked of us that we be perfect to enter into greater truths; but we must have the willingness to continue to perfect ourselves. "Every day something must be achieved inwardly. Often it is only a slight accomplishment, but it must be pursued with iron determination and unwavering will."[34]

To recognize the exercises that we need requires of us an honest evaluation of how we respond to life, what capacities we do have, and what capacities we are lacking. Our response to our life shows us this. We may have recognized ourselves in the descriptions of the soul activities given in the other chapters, and this may indicate the area to focus on. It is not always so clear because as adults we are able to cover up tendencies and prevent their outer expression, even though they still exist. We sometimes convince ourselves that certain tendencies don't exist, when in fact they have a great deal of power inwardly. Only true and honest self-evaluation is useful.

By reading through and understanding these following exercises you will perceive the path and your own next steps more clearly. It is not meant that you attempt all the exercises at once, but rather to find where you are and work with that. It is most useful to begin with one of the sentient soul exercises and then add others as you see appropriate. If you find that you are already through the first stages, you can begin to look toward the harder exercises as the starting point. We need to pass through all stages; skipping a stage is never useful. It would be like skipping a milestone in childhood. At the same time, one sheath does not require complete change before the next can be worked with.

The Sentient Soul; Purifying the Desire Body

The ego first takes hold of the sentient soul. "If the passions, instincts, desires from which the sentient soul must be cleansed before the intellectual soul can strive for truth, come into it, they will prevent one from getting away from oneself, and will keep the ego tied to a fixed viewpoint."[35] The clearest way to do this is through inner schooling exercises that work specifically on the various challenges of taking hold of this desire body. This leads to a positive use of the sentient soul capacities. We can understand and gain an experience of the positive activity of this soul sheath through following the inner activity of the color red.

Imagine the color red, immersing yourself entirely in this light-filled vibrant color. Inwardly feel the inner activity as though you are united with this red consciousness. Here we can have an inner experience of the sentient soul activity. Try to use words that tell of your experience to describe the red activity. Red evokes something similar to the inner qualities of strength, vitality, determination, passion, activity, power, and force.

These positive qualities continue because they are necessary activities in serving life; but it is the particular personal soul preferences that need transforming, that bind us to serving the personal self. Here following are seven exercises that free the sentient soul and strengthen its inner capacities.

EXERCISE 1. Purify certain wishes, comforts, and pleasures.

The important aspect of this exercise is that the things you choose to transform must be thought through clearly. Do not choose based on society's preferences; do not choose based on vanity or pride, or all the other ego-enhancing reasons to suppress certain wishes, comforts, and pleasures. Rather, make the choice clearly and independently out of yourself

You choose because you recognize how chasing your wishes, pleasures, and comforts makes you unfree. You see how the comfort draws you into unconsciousness, acting like a large nipple that you suck on to escape being awake and aware. You recognize that the pleasure amplifies the personal preferences for how life should be; and that the wishes diminish your trust that your soul's true needs will be met.

A. *Purifying wishes* means not allowing your soul to dream into wanting what you do not have. Fantasizing about a future that will satisfy your personal wants for this life, needs to be suppressed. It is interesting to see how this wishing consciousness sets up future pain or future elation. This is a trap of the personality, setting the stage for the highs and lows of the drama of life, which becomes all of our own making and all our own creation. The wishing consciousness gives us a feeling of success if it works in our favor, and a feeling of failure if it doesn't. It gives the illusion that the control is in our hands. It diminishes our inner trust in what life needs to unfold for us.

B. *Purifying pleasures* means suppressing the personal desires of how life is pleasurable or not pleasurable to you. We all have preferences that make our lives more or less pleasurable, according to whether they are fulfilled or not. They often limit our choices and interfere with the unfolding of what might have been if we had not controlled the situation with our preferences. Wanting to seek pleasure and avoid pain sometimes becomes so limiting that we don't allow life to happen. We try to stop life from expressing itself, and want life only to express our desires. We do this, from the little things, such as where we will sit in the restaurant to feel at ease, to the major things, such as being interested in partnering only with someone who has a certain income. You may not relate to these examples; but we all need to find our individual pleasures that rule us and consciously stop them from ruling.

C. *Purifying comforts* can be the hardest exercise because we often use our comforts to soothe our pains, or to reward ourselves for enduring difficulties, which we can feel we are enduring just by being alive. When we look carefully at what takes place, we may recognize that in fact we are trying to become more unconscious, more asleep. There is a part of our being that does not want to wake up or evolve into the future, but would rather return unconsciously to the spiritual world and be rocked like a babe in the arms of God. Our comforts are all the ways we reward ourselves when things have been difficult, and all the ways we cushion the blows to soothe ourselves. Being comfortable has become the necessity of the civilized world, making comfort a basic need that we all now demand.

In this exercise we choose one comfort that we see as having this effect of supporting unconsciousness; then we first start with that. This will help in two ways: by strengthening our inner capacities and by revealing how many other comforts we use without even being aware we are doing so.

These three obvious attachments of the sentient soul may seem too simple to be exercises of self-development; but like all exercises given out of the esoteric schooling they have far-reaching possibilities. These three are spoken about in the deep and profound work *Light on the Path*, which Steiner recommended to awaken the higher I. The first three aphorisms implore the student to kill out ambition, desire of life, and desire of comfort. What will become of our passions and our drives when all that drove us is extinguished? If we do not have the carrot of desire dangling in front of us, what will call us to work onward?

At first this inner change may feel like the plug has been pulled out of our drive for life; but through this schooling the soul is not weakened, but strengthened. The fourth aphorism confirms that these forces are not extinguished permanently, but there is a change of direction regarding who they are serving. The instruction says to work as those work who are ambitious. Respect life as those do who desire it. Be happy, as those are who live for happiness. This ability to work with the power of the ambitious person but without personal ambition is a new freedom. "The killing of all selfness is the foundation for the higher life, for whoever destroys selfness lives in eternal being."[36] The soul still uses the force, but uses it on behalf of the Spirit.

EXERCISE 2. Hold back all antipathy and sympathy toward both those who hurt you in the past and those who favored you.

One way of working with this is to call to mind inwardly, as vividly as possible, the individual that in the past hurt you or favored you. In order to re-engage the soul hook, we need to rebuild circumstances in picture form. Imagine where the hurt or favor took place. What time of year was it? What time of day was it? Picture what you were wearing; what the person was wearing; what all the outer circumstances were. As much as possible, rebuild the external picture that took place. Then attempt to look only objectively upon this person, quieting all inner responses to the hurt or the favor that happened. Quiet all your internal reactions, and simply look on as though the hurt or the favor had nothing to do with you.

We may notice that we are happy to renounce the insult as having nothing to do with us, but perhaps not so happy to renounce the favor. This is one of the important reasons why people struggle to take hold of the sentient soul. They still want to hold onto the positive stroking that comes from others, and in doing so they also hold onto the doorway to the hurt. This is an important evaluation to make in our internal struggle to overcome many things. We want half of the coin—we want to hold onto the parts we like, the gratification; but not the parts we don't like. Surrendering both is essential. Recognizing the part that refuses to give up the strokes is a key.

For some, insult is more familiar biographically, and praise is unfamiliar or awkward. And so, strangely, insult is more gratifying than praise. On a deep unconscious level of wanting to repeat the known, the pain becomes the stroking. Seeing both and giving up both is necessary.

EXERCISE 3. Look at something you are intending to do and bring up all the pros and cons of this intention.

This is important because you must be able to bring up objections to your own choices, if you are to be able to assess where these things come from in yourself. The sentient soul can have an intention to do something that springs from personal preferences alone. This leads to a self-will that separates us further from our higher intentions; instead, it contributes to our particular self. Again, this simple exercise has far-reaching possibilities for our transformation. "If you act as a separate being you lock yourself out of the closed chains of world action, you cut yourself out. If you act in the spirit, you live into universal world action."[37]

For this exercise, you need to choose one thing at a time to evaluate. Choose one thing you have decided to do. Then make a list on paper or in your mind of all the pros you can think of for doing it; and then a list of all the cons. You will not only strengthen yourself, but you will see what was pulling the strings of the decision to do this thing.

Many times we do not look at the motivator in us. We choose what suits our past conditioning or our wants, without thinking of the ripple effects of our actions. This can be a way of avoiding full responsibility for our actions. We often wish to avoid owning the consequences of our actions. Working with this exercise can be an insight into many of our ways of avoiding ownership of our decisions. We can't change what we don't own.

EXERCISE 4. Avoid taking the advice of others.

We often believe that others know better, especially in our times when there is so much information that we can't know everything. Of course, we can look to other sources for information; however, we will develop at a greater rate in strength for our inner life if we do not accept another's advice, but rather listen to, consider, weigh, and evaluate what others have to say in relationship to what we already know and understand for ourselves. This is a very different gesture from unthinkingly adopting someone's advice about what you should or shouldn't do, feel, or think.

Placing another in authority in your inner life weakens the authority of your own ego to take hold of yourself. This, of course, does not mean closing oneself off from others or the world, such as never reading a book or attending a lecture. But it does mean working with the content, actively engaging yourself with what you have read or heard. Observe where the differences of thought lie; where you can take in and extend, develop, or transform the thoughts.

Again this simple exercise has far-reaching consequences in spiritual development. When I meet another, something new comes into being; when two or more gather something new is created. In the meeting of the sunrays and an object, an image arises as a living process between these two things uniting. When I am present and engaged in learning, something new is born. The new that is arising is always in the present; and the spirit works in the now. In the present, something comes into being; a third activity through the meeting of the two.

This is a secret of deep inner work. Active souls can learn from anyone and any situation because of what they bring to meet it. The creative spirit works in the present moment. The present in us activates this creativity. I must bring myself to the world; through this meeting the new can arise. "Good is something that is creative in the world-all; something that is arising and coming into being. The good is the creator of continual cosmic births, great and small. "[38]

EXERCISE 5. Give up ninety-nine percent of your personal judgments.

First we have to see and be aware of how many personal judgments we have, which continually stream in our thinking, affecting our feeling, and in turn, our actions.

These judgments are our scaffolding of selfness. They are constructed through the outer life, the life we have led up until this present moment. We rarely recognize our continual judging of the world based on past conditioning. As soon as we judge something it is fixed, finished, and held in a place. The world of the spirit is full of living consciousness. For living thoughts, judgment is death. We need so little of these judgments to live our life. They are the death of our thinking.

Personal judgments are mortal. They have no place in spiritual activity, and eventually they all must die. When we are reborn again to a different time, race, or religion, with all its new conditioning, we will receive a new scaffolding of judgments; a new mortal veil to view life through. To be liberated from this veil brings us closer to the immortal self. "To the extent we have let selfness die in us we are immortal. Selfness is what is mortal in us. This is the true meaning of the saying 'If you don't die before you die, when you die you rot.' "[39] Only the immortal in us continues to live on in our journey beyond the sense world.

EXERCISE 6. Do not allow yourself to find distress in circumstances that are distressing to you personally.

This is a challenging exercise, because it is difficult for us to look upon some situations and not be distressed. In some ways it requires obedience toward the wisdom of the spiritual world. And it is difficult not to be in inner rebellion to what we perceive in our own lives or in the lives of others.

At the same time we can strive not to fall into a passive resignation about what is happening, believing it cannot be influenced by those present. It is said that only the obedient ones can lift the fallen and soothe the sick.

Recently on a plane journey I was given yet another opportunity to work with this. A father and his four-year-old son were sitting behind me, and the young boy was drawing pictures. The boy said, "I want to draw a picture for mommy." The father responded, "This is our time; this is not your time with mommy, and it hurts me when you talk about her in our time." The child began to cry, and kept saying, "I want to draw a picture for mommy." They kept fighting back and forth until the father then said distressingly, "You're hurting me, and if you keep speaking about mommy I will tell you how mean she is, how she hurts me, how she lies. I will tell you about all the nasty things that your mother does, and that she is a bad and terrible person." The child was becoming more distressed.

This could have been distressing to me personally, and I could have gone into battle with this father from a personal response. Or I could have evaluated the situation as karmic, and sat wondering why this child required such circumstances, perhaps refraining from action out of resignation. Instead, I recognized there was something that I could bring. That the father and the son sitting were behind me on that flight was my karma also.

I turned around and spoke to the father, explaining that I am an educator who trains teachers in their work with children. I told him that the child was not trying to hurt him, but that probably because it was dinnertime the child began recalling the usual rhythm in the day, and that included his mother. I described to him how the consciousness of a four-year-old works in pictures, and that every time the father said, "Don't talk about mommy," the child was picturing, "Talk about mommy." In fact he was engaging the child's consciousness more strongly in the direction of mommy by his use of language. I mentioned how if the father used this idea that the child was seeing everything he said, he would recognize how his own consciousness was amplifying the situation.

Gratefully the father immediately took my suggestion, and the next time the child said, "I want to draw a picture for mommy," the father replied, "Let's draw a picture for grandmother." When the child said, "I miss my mommy," the father responded, "We are going to see grandmother because it's her birthday, and it's going to be so much fun." A little later all was calm in the seats behind.

Later in the flight, the child ripped up a picture the father had drawn for him; the father asked, "Why did you rip my picture?" And the child replied, "I wanted you to feel what it's like to be ripped up the way you've been ripping me up." I thought he had a great point, and inwardly gave a little cheer that he could put that out so clearly. Between us, the father learned something useful. The potentially distressing situation was an opportunity for intervention. We could all become paralyzed by distress; but every distressing situation may be a call to action.

I have come to the frightening conclusion that I am the decisive element. It is my personal approach that creates the climate. It is my daily mood that makes the weather. I possess tremendous power to make life miserable or joyous. I can be a tool of torture or an instrument of inspiration; I can humiliate or humor, hurt or heal. In all situations, it is my response that decides whether a crisis is escalated or de-escalated, and a person is humanized or dehumanized. If we treat people only as they are, we make them worse. If we treat people as they ought to be, we help them become what they are capable of becoming.

—J. W. von Goethe

EXERCISE 7. Work with anger.

Anger is often a call to defend the self; to defend my way, my opinion, my wants. But it can also be a call to develop the right kind of self-possession. Individuals need to be able to stand the ground between self—what we believe to be right, to be truth in the world—and what we see outside ourselves as error or untruths. When our anger rises to defend our personal position, we waste its power on defending the particular self. However, we can be called to defend another person or a truth. To be able to stand in defense of a truth requires a self-possession that the transformation of anger can give us.

As mentioned in the last exercise, when on the airplane I began to hear the father ripping up his child, there was a welling of force in me to defend the child. I could have angrily addressed the father. But this would have been defending my opinion and myself in some way. Anger externalized on the other is defending the one who is angry. Instead, I needed to use that force to stand strong and turn to meet the situation. Without aggression but with firm boundaries, what could have been anger (and in fact, a loss of true connection with myself) became a sense of self that could generate action into the world.

Anger, when it is used to give a boundary to the soul, becomes strength to encounter the world and not be influenced by the errors that are trying to win that moment. Such strength can be used in the service of the great battle. But as it says in *The Light on the Path*, your personal self must stand aside. "Stand aside in the coming battle,

83

and of those thou fightest be not thou the warrior. Look for the warrior and let him fight in thee."[40]

We cannot completely suppress what lives in us, for this leads to a distortion of the forces. We can overcome the grip and the lack of freedom anger places on us. "Overcoming something does not mean shirking or shunning it. It is a strange sort of sacrifice that is made by those who propose to cast off their passionate self by evading it. Instead of trying to evade such emotions, we must transmute them in ourselves. Transmuted anger is love in action."[41]

The Intellectual Soul; Seeking the Truth

Inwardly, the intellectual soul works differently; it is slightly more below the threshold of consciousness. Taking hold of the intellectual soul requires penetrating the etheric body and the habits that live there. "An honest striving for the truth leads to human understanding; but the love of truth for the sake of one's own personality leads to intolerance and destruction of other people's freedom."[42]

This inner activity is attuned more to the color yellow; when we immerse ourselves in a vibrant yellow color imagination, we can experience certain inner activities. These processes may be given experience-words such as striving for wisdom, intelligence, clarity, expansion, joy. These qualities of the intellectual soul continue to be active in our inner life. The habitual nature that limits us is transformed through taking hold of certain soul exercises. Here are five such exercises that work to develop capacities and liberate old habitual forms, and in doing so, vitalize our forces.

EXERCISE 1. Check your thinking.

It has been stated several times before how thinking can become habitual; how we place onto the world the thoughts that live in us, instead of trying to receive the thoughts that live in things. Most things that we see in the outer world have a reason, a thought behind them. Learning to enter into the thought that is behind an action is a beginning in learning to let things speak to us. For instance, imagine that your neighbor has done something like put the garbage bin out three days before the garbage collection usually happens. You could just think she must be going away, because that's the only reason you have put the garbage bin out early in the past. We jump to conclusions out of our past experience.

The reality could have been that your neighbor has hurt his arm, and was unable to put the bin out himself; so when a family member was visiting, he asked her to put the bin out.

Whatever action takes place in the world, there has been a thought preceding the action. We could say that the thought still lives; and if we are able, we can re-experience the thought behind things. We connect to the thought that lives, not to our own limited thinking.

In this exercise you will need to check your thinking; and strange as it may seem, you would need to check with your neighbor (or with someone) about why the bin went out three days early. If it correlates with your thinking, all well and good. However, if there is another reason that is different from what you thought, you have to find where you made the mistake. Did you project your past upon the present? Did you make assumptions based on logic alone? Once you have found your mistake, you must then inwardly and pictorially adjust your thinking until it is in line with the actual events.

This exercise can also be worked in the opposite direction. Imagine a child at school who appears tired and out of sorts. Something has led to the child's being this way, and you try to think through what might have happened. Did the child have a restless night? Were there disturbances in the home? Once again, you have to check your thinking by following up with the adults to find out what really occurred. If you are correct, and you were able to follow through with your thoughts into the past in the right way, then all is well and good. We must beware not to boost our egos because we have the correct thinking, because this would cause more hurdles. If your conclusions were not right, then you have to adjust your thinking pictorially again until your thoughts have aligned with the truth of what happened. Strengthening our thinking in this way, we begin to glimpse the true nature of thought and the immense capacity that lives untapped in us. "It is not merely I who think, for it thinks me. World-becoming expresses itself in me, and my soul provides only the stage upon which the world lives as thought."[43]

EXERCISE 2. Overcoming something habitual.

This exercise is unlike the will exercises in the six sub-
sidiary exercises, because we are not initiating something
new; rather, we are overcoming a habit that already exists. We need to choose something deeply habitual and
stop doing it.

This has far-reaching consequences not only in the inner
life, but even in our life forces. There was once a case I
knew of involving the question of diet. A woman suffered
from lack of energy and excess mucus in the mornings;
she wondered if it was something she was allergic to. The
doctor enquired into her diet, and learned she had a very
rigid habitual diet. The doctor did one thing: he suggested that half an hour before she ate her usual break-
fast (which she had eaten for thirty years or more), she
should instead eat one apple.

The changes were substantial; she had more energy
and less mucus. The apple did not do this. In our intellectual minds we may think the apple made the difference, but it was the change of habit. The consciousness
that was required for this particular woman to change
her diet supported the ego's entering into her habit life
and adjusting it.

Because of our materialistic thinking, many people
assume it is the food that causes the change. The reality is
that the removing of gluten and dairy products from the
diet requires a continual activity of will. The ego cannot
allow the normal habits of eating; it has to be conscious
at each meal. This wakefulness has substantial effects on

the individual's underactive metabolism. Materialistic thinking assumes that the problem was the gluten and the dairy. The problem was the sleepy, unstimulated habitual metabolic system. This doctor said, "All diets work for about three months; they work until they become a habit."

It is not the food; it is the change of habit. One of the great problems we face when we believe it is the food, is that removing the food rarely strengthens our metabolism. If the food presents an obstacle to cure, then it is possible that reducing its consumption for a short period of time is necessary; but most commonly we need to strengthen our capacity to overcome the food. We need to develop the metabolic force to transform the food, rather than with-draw it altogether. I have had many cases where people gave up certain foods. For three months it seemed to work for them, but then the symptoms came back. And they gave up more foods, and eventually they were living on a minimal selection of the great smorgasbord of possibilities.

It seems to be similar with taking synthesized vita-mins and minerals; we spoon-feed our digestive system, which may be essential for short periods of time when the source is inadequate, or the digestion itself is unable to extract the vitamins and minerals. In the long run, this weakens the digestive capacity by spoon-feeding nutri-tion and leaving the metabolic system lying on the couch. Nutrition arises not only from what we eat, but also out of overcoming the food we take in. In digestion, we dena-ture the qualities of the food and use the building blocks to create our own individualized protein and energy, which we will use in an individual way. The whole process of nutrition is an image that depicts how the human being progresses in body, soul, and spirit.

All things in the world need to be met, need to be overcome, transformed, and used for the advancement of humanity. The stronger the metabolic system, the easier it is to receive our nourishment from the plant world. The metabolic system is strengthened by the power of the soul, not just the physical body. This is one reason that strong souls often do not require a meat diet. Another is that the astral element of the meat does not resonate with the individual when the astral element in the person has been purified. Of course, this is not a recommendation to change to a vegetarian diet; however, sometimes the body continues habits of eating when they are no longer strengthening to the individual's needs.

If you stop eating meat and the body suffers, the metabolic system still needs the ease of nutrition it gains from this food. If, on the other hand, the soul suffers, and you feel deprived and longing for meat, then the soul still wants what is familiar to its activity. And it is "better to eat meat than think meat." Often the ideologically forced vegetarians end up consuming vast quantities of legumes, which Steiner said has a polluting effect on the etheric body. This is especially the case with lentils and soy products; these food substances draw in the nitrogenous forces that are a sign of the attempted astralization of the plant. The plant tries to become animal-like in its activity. Within the human digestion, these forces, in excess, increase the hardening sclerotic processes in the body.

EXERCISE 3. Change your way of walking or writing.

The way a human being walks or writes is an expression of the deep conditioning in the etheric body. Sometimes you can see this in people who have gone through the changes of huge weight loss. They continue to walk as though they have obese bodies, even though their weight has changed. Their old walk will make it harder for them to hold off the weight because the heavy body pattern continues to be expressed in their movement.

It is hard for us to understand just how our walk affects our physical, etheric, and astral bodies. You can try this yourself by entering into the walk of another person. You can begin to see how different life would be if you walked that way.

It is interesting to see how the temperaments expressed through the etheric body are also reflected in our walking. A person with a choleric temperament walks hard, heels down, head first into the world. We can hear them coming, chin forward, marching. People with a sanguine temperament have a kind of changeable walk; there seems to be little rhythm, and odd or random gestures appear in the limbs. The phlegmatic person leads from the belly, like water meandering through the world at a harmonious pace, whereas the person with a melancholic temperament is heavily pulled down and weighted by the body.

Slipping into the walk of another is a very useful exercise. Train stations with long walkways are great practice grounds for this. By slipping into the walk of others we begin to become more aware of our own walk. Making a conscious decision to change our walk is a consistent and constant exercise.

It will take many months of practice to alter a habit that may have been there since our childhood. You will even be able to notice in many adults the habit of movement from their childhood. This habit of movement has an effect on the capacity for change on many levels of our being.

Individuals who are more metabolic-dominant may gain a lot from changing their walk or other gross motor activities. Those who are more nerve-sense dominant may gain more from changing their handwriting, because they tend toward the fixed, fine motor skills such as handwriting forms.

EXERCISE 4. Change unhealthy habits.

What is an unhealthy habit? Picking one's nose? Leaving the toilet seat up? All so-called bad manners? Whatever you choose to change, do not pick one of the socially conditioned habits, for this is not productive in the deep work of self-transformation.

An unhealthy habit is one that separates you from the truth. How can a habit separate us from the truth? Our thinking affects our feeling, which in turn affects our actions. If our thinking is erroneous, then our actions will be; it will follow that our actions are also untrue. To find the unhealthy habit, we must trace our actions and our feelings back to the original belief in thought life.

Take a habit you may have that is detrimental to your progression, such as the need to be right. This habit may mean that you are waiting to interject your opinions as much as possible. It may mean that you are in a sort of competition with others even if they don't know about it; ready to express how right you are and how much you know. This is a habit worth changing. It affects your thoughts, your feeling life, and perhaps even how you breathe. This need to be right has become a habit, and must be dismantled. We must think through this habit to understand its origin. At one point in your life it may have served a purpose; it may have allowed you to be apart of your family habits. Everything that separates us from a connection with the present moment and present needs, separates us from the living streaming spiritual activity. This spiritual activity allows us to give what is needed in the moment. To respond toward the progression of others and ourselves supports freedom.

EXERCISE 5. Interest in whatever you are learning.

Unfortunately in our time we are commonly asked to learn things that we don't wish to learn, that we have no interest in. In order to gain certain qualifications we often have to cram our minds with thoughts that do not interest us. This practice has a negative effect on us as human beings, and especially on our health-giving forces.

For the whole human being there is hardly anything worse than being far away in the soul, with one's heart, from what the head must perform. This not only goes against the nature of a finer, more sensitive person, but also influences the strength of the etheric body to the highest degree...... The more people have to do what does not interest them, the weaker they make their ether bodies.[44]

If we find ourselves in this position, it is important to bring interest into whatever we are learning and doing. Even if we can't find interest in the subject itself, we can be interested in the effects of what we are learning. Often high school students complain that they have to learn things in school that they are going to completely disregard when they leave school. I often suggest to them that they use this opportunity to develop their will capacity, and to see how they can gain some sort of mastery over themselves. This painful experience of the teenagers often feels like their will moving in reverse. Many young people experience this. They have an assignment they need to do, and all they can do is lie on the bed empty-headed, unable to move, unable to engage themselves. This expression of the anxiety of the intellectual soul is difficult to carry. The other expression of anxiety is more obvious. They are the students who cram themselves full of information, anxiously trying to know more and more. These young people often burn out, or get Brain Fag syndrome before they reach college or university. In their soul life, both groups are disinterested toward the content they have to take in. One group can't move and is blocked, while the other is overly cramming information.

Interest is what connects us to the things we need to take in. Interest engages our thinking, feeling, and will. Engaging the wholeness of our inner life prevents the content from becoming merely information. Knowledge arises not out of the thing we need to take in, but through our connection to it. Interest is our connector.

The Consciousness Soul; Seeking Beyond Ourselves

The I takes hold of the consciousness soul in a way that is different from the sentient soul and the intellectual soul. If we immerse ourselves in a color imagination, we can experience the difference the color blue inwardly expresses. The activity of the vibrant blue qualities could be described as peace, or humility, or devotion. The following three exercises are educators of the consciousness soul. "The will can be penetrated by a force that goes out toward the supersensible unknown. This quality of will, which enables one to wish to carry out one's aims and intentions with regard to the unknown, is devotion."[45]

EXERCISE 1. Strengthen memory.

In this exercise we attempt regularly to strengthen our memory by using picture consciousness. The first example: whenever you place your keys down in the house you try to recall exactly, in a picture, all that was there where you placed them. Memorize the small table, the other little things on the table, where the table is positioned in the hall, and so forth. Of course you cannot use any habits, because if you always place your keys on the table in the hall, this would not act as a memory exercise. Each day put the keys in a different place. And each morning try to recall where they were placed, through recalling the picture of where they are now. You are not trying to trick yourself, but rather to strengthen your picture-remembering consciousness.

Our picture consciousness is the doorway to the imagination soul; when we think in pictures we are developing an inner capacity that is essential for spiritual activity. Pictures engage the thinking, feeling, and the will, all together. They create wholeness in the inner life, and through this wholeness, a doorway to spiritual activity.

EXERCISE 2. Presence

In this exercise we try to recall a past event in all its detail. For example, you think about the friend that you spoke with two weeks ago in the street. Where did you meet? What were you wearing? What was the other person wearing? What was the conversation about? You may not be able to recall all the details; in that case, you add the details yourself. For instance you may have forgotten what color the friend's shirt was, so make sure to add the detail of the color of the shirt. You may not have remembered how you ended the conversation; nevertheless, you continue to create the whole picture of the encounter, filling in yourself all the details that you missed, recalling in picture form all the details that you can recall. If we do this exercise each day about something in the past (yesterday, a week ago, a month ago, even a year ago), eventually we will find that our capacity to recall is strengthened because our presence is strengthened. It is astounding how much we can recall when we are mindful in this picture-consciousness way. This will in time lead to greater and greater presence in every encounter.

It is in the presence of the moment that we recognize the direct workings of the spirit. In the spiritual world, behind every picture is a living consciousness, a spiritual activity. As we learn to live in the world of pictures, we slowly become aware of the presences behind the appearance of things. It is not the capacity to recall what is external that becomes important, but that through that capacity we begin to see what else is living in every meeting with another.

EXERCISE 3. Reverence

Practicing reverence does not come easily to the consciousness soul in our times. Reverence means raising our soul toward the higher in all things, in all other people, and even in situations. From this we can try to enter lovingly into another person's higher qualities. This attitude cannot be artificially induced; it almost arises by itself from insight into the spiritual nature of the world. But reverence can be sought after; we can bring effort to seeking the eternal that lives in things. This effort supports our practice of devotion and reverence in our thinking. Showing respect outwardly to another is not enough; we need to hold this respect in our thoughts, while eliminating any disrespectful or diminishing thoughts. "The soul is drawn by the strength of its reverence toward the eternal, with which it belongs, to unite itself."[46] Training ourselves in the mood of devotion and reverence reveals what is worthy of reverence.

It is said that the gods have placed willpower before the gates of knowledge, and they require it before allowing entry. Willpower is strengthened in all these exercises. They also offer more: we can gain much insight into the future path of deeper inner work by considering and penetrating these exercises. Even if we do not work with all the exercises, all reveal something far deeper than appears at first.

In the unfolding of the inner path, we circle around, moving to successively deeper levels. The level of training that we begin now will provide substance for the future. This can help us distinguish between true inner work exercises, and those that are produced to satisfy the soul's preferences.

Various other non-schooling exercises have been developed to so-called help people cope with life. For instance, some ways of looking and assessing our biographies are given in counseling techniques to help us manage our life. For example, it is common for people to be counseled in learning to get their needs met by others; learning to be clear about their needs and communicating them in a way others can hear. They learn sometimes even to have a facilitator to make sure they are heard, and that their requests are registered. We may be taught things like putting our own needs first, and call this self-love.

Many of these so-called counseling or social management/education techniques will need to be eliminated if the student is to progress in higher development. Such techniques are very different from the exercises that support genuine self-development that will lead to initiation preparation.

The beginning exercises that are set out here can produce high results on the true path. They are passed on through initiates who see the great journey of humanity through the course of time. The results can be seen as essential for higher transformation.

It is of utmost importance to see what needs to be worked on by evaluating yourself, and by assessing each of these exercises out of yourself. However, the true self, or, as Rumi says, "the friend," has been continuously assisting you with this task throughout your adult life. It is possible to assess your adult life from the point of view of the true self, which is working to school you through the outer events of your life. Then, by our inner responses, not the outer events, we evaluate and assess what the true I has been encouraging us to transform.

We can also assess our resistance to this transformation by honestly evaluating our responses to the outer circumstances of our biography. Did we change and develop in ourselves from these outer events, or have we amplified our particular personal self? The true I, in the events of our biography, is schooling each of us toward the highest development that we can achieve. The inner work exercises help us to transform ourselves and meet life as a schooling.

There are beautiful wild forces within us.
Let them turn the mills inside.

– Francis of Assisi[47]

We face three kinds of resistance to self-development. The first is our own lethargy. Lethargy is not only a lack of will or enthusiasm, but also can feel like a powerful pull in the opposite direction of our intentions. Sometimes just deciding to do an exercise will then engage the first resistance. It is like those who decide to give up smoking, and find they smoke even more than before the decision was made. Lethargy is overcome in the very doing of the exercise. But if you think you will have a great resistance, then start with something you know is achievable, not taking on too much too quickly. The capacity developed through overcoming this first resistance is known as self-control leading to self-confidence. It is a necessary requirement for further stages of transformation. It is very different from the confidence of the ambitious person or one who has achievements in the outer world. It is genuine confidence to govern oneself.

The second resistance is feeling that you are "fighting yourself through a dense thicket." Once we begin the exercise in order to transform, so does the battle to stay the same begin; the path seems denser and harder than we originally thought. What appeared to be a small exercise has called up a mighty resistance, and the task of change can appear too difficult. But it is the small steps of trying again and again that strengthen us, and eventually clear the way. The overcoming of this second resistance leads to what is called self-reliance in the esoteric schooling. This is the ability to rely on the forces within. These forces within will assist you through the challenges that arise on the path.

The third resistance is to the pain of the change. As we enter the thicket we feel the scrapes and struggles; it is uncomfortable and often painful. It is often said in the esoteric schools that higher knowledge is attainable only through pain, and it is here that we encounter the pain. It is the pain of our own resistance. The capacity that is developed here is obedience. This obedience is without inner rebellion toward the path that needs to be trod, knowing that the suffering is the purification of our own resistance.

It is most interesting that those who go before us carve the path that we can walk. However, because the path is there we are called to walk it. If we resist it, we usually suffer. We are all called to raise ourselves to the level of the collective consciousness of the times. In our times this is the consciousness soul. It will be by inner effort, or through sickness and suffering, that we achieve all the steps necessary to develop fully the consciousness soul. The evolution that has preceded us has a momentum, a pull, and it becomes a necessity that we can't hold back. We can choose to take the path consciously, or life will call us until we take it.

The future development of humanity is an open choice, the unwritten pages of humanity's future. This will be worked upon through initiation and the sacrifice that individuals undertake as they work to clear the way for others. They can do this only through the strengthened I. The I is first strengthened through taking hold of all that lives in the personal soul. "We begin to be no longer wholly in harmony with our own human personality; and when we experience this to an ever greater extent, much has been achieved in the furtherance of higher spiritual experience."[48] Our own limited personality becomes like a bad housemate we have to keep sharing with, even though we recognize all the things we would rather not have to live with.

When we enter into initiation, our suffering becomes a choice that we enter into gladly. We know that it is the battle of the finite particular self with the infinite spiritual self, and that only the truth of the spirit is of lasting importance.

4

THE INITIATION OF THE I AND THE SPIRITUAL WORLD

The I is strengthened through the great task of taking hold of all that lives in the soul of the individual and liberating the forces from the soul's body-bound activity. This strengthening is essential for the next step in development, the initiation of the I. The first preliminary step in the initiation is the separation of the sheath I (the ego) from the higher I. All the capacities developed through taking hold of the soul are now divided between the everyday ego and the newborn higher spiritual I. If there is not adequate strength to serve both, the ego will become overwhelmed by the remainder of the untransformed soul activities. This can lead to great instability in everyday life; the ego's capacity to direct the soul is diminished in a way that may prove truly disturbing. "If human beings have not attained firmness in moral judgment; if they have not gained sufficient control over their inclinations, instincts, and passions, then they will make their ordinary ego independent in a state in which these soul powers act."[49]

It is important to know that it is not the ego (the sheath I), that is initiated; it is the newborn higher I that takes this path. The higher I has been endowed with the strength gained from the ego's work of individualizing.

There needs to be a certain ground and a definite relationship to transforming at least one of the soul sheaths before the higher I can be called toward an initiation that leads to a free relationship with the spiritual world. "It is of greatest importance that students of the spiritual have acquired a quite definite soul state when they become conscious of a newborn ego."[50]

This strength is essential for the health of the sheath I as it holds the daily life, and for the higher I, which needs to have the capacity to continue the initiation steps. It is always a destiny question whether or not an individual will be offered this path of the initiation of the I. As St. Teresa of Avila expressed:

No one can near God unless he has
prepared a bed for
you.
A thousand souls hear his call every second,
but most everyone then looks into their life's mirror
and says, "I am not worthy to leave this
sadness."[51]

Even though this initiation is not determined by us, we can do the work of being ready for it through taking hold of what lives in us. This work produces results that take effect in our daily lives, even if we are not called at this stage toward higher initiation steps. No efforts are lost; all have their effects on human progress. On the initiation path we experience the truth of the spiritual life directly. Through the preparation of taking hold of what lives in us, we receive more readily what flows toward us from the spiritual world into our everyday experiences.

The initiation path begins with the preparation toward crossing the threshold between this external world of sense and the non-sense perceptible worlds. This crossing is prepared for, just as birth into the earthly sense world is prepared for. The gestational months support the developing of the physical organs that allow for life on earth to be experienced fully. Likewise, the spiritual organs are prepared for in the gestation time before crossing the threshold, so that the crossing can be fruitful. The spiritual organs arise from the transformed soul sheaths. We all make this crossing at death; the initiate makes this crossing in life. Initiation allows those who are now born consciously into the world of spirit to see the living reality behind the so-called world of appearance.

This path will lead to a direct and conscious relationship with the living spiritual world. Yet even those who are not called to this path at this time need to begin to relate to the truth of their essential nature.

Humanity must develop awareness of not being of this earth; and this must grow stronger and stronger. In future, human beings must walk on the earth who say to themselves, "Yes, at birth I enter into a physical body, but this is a transitional stage. I really remain in the spiritual world. I am conscious that only part of my sensory nature is united with the earth, and that I do not leave the world where I am between death and rebirth with the whole of my essential nature."[52]

In the purely spiritual world the laws are different than the laws in our earthly world; there is no division between oneself and what one is experiencing. If one perceives a picture, the picture is internal, not external, as it is in the sense world. If one has an experience of spiritual activity, the activity is within and not outside. If one encounters a being spiritually, there is no division; there is unity. In the earthly world, only our capacity for thinking comes close to this non-duality. When we are completely immersed inwardly in an active, dynamic thought process, we can lose the sense of duality. In the earthly world, will-filled thinking is closest to this spiritual activity. In the spiritual world, this complete immersion is real to our whole being. Our ability to experience this arises from transforming the soul sheaths, so that we may see, hear, and touch the spiritual reality. Through this preparation, the soul sheaths are developed and transformed to become organs of perception for the spirit, just as the physical senses are organs of perception for the soul.

It is difficult to describe the nature of seeing or hearing in the spiritual world because the language that belongs to the sense world does not do it justice. In "seeing" in the spiritual world, you are at the same time both the consciousness that sees and that which is seen by the consciousness. The other's thought is your thought; it is a thought that you are not divided from. Common thinking is a divided activity, but in the spiritual world you are thought. The outer world is in you, but there is no personal witness of this because there is no inside or outside. All is Self, and yet there is no personal self knowing this.

True Clairvoyance

The consciousness soul is bound primarily to the physical body. It has an intimate relationship with all that comes from the spiritual world and lives behind the substance of the physical body. Transformed, the consciousness soul forces become the *Imagination Soul* in the spiritual world.

Through the imagination soul, the non-sense perceptible world can be "seen." It is also through these eyes that individual karma is recognized. Once having seen all that belongs to us personally, all that has taken place in our past, the subjective eyes are cleared. Then the soul can be aware of the objective cosmic activities that make the imprints in the elemental substance. It is here that all the past imprints live, or all that has been in all of human evolution. This is sometimes referred to as the Akashic Record, which the initiates access to illuminate their teachings.

Developing the imagination soul means that the spirit has the clairvoyant capacity to see all that is spiritual behind the physical appearance. This clairvoyant capacity develops through an initiation that can be bestowed only if the destiny of the individual requires it. This is not a path for the majority of humanity at this stage of human development. Developing the imagination soul is not the same as receiving imaginations this side of the threshold in our daily life or in our inner contemplative space. These imaginations are mediated by the sentient soul in the form of inner pictures, thoughts, and words.

All of humanity is now at the stage of being able to receive imaginations from the spiritual world. Many people have the experience of receiving an imagination or an insight inwardly. A teacher could be struggling with what to do for a child in the class. During the teacher's inner contemplation or thinking, an inner picture, thought, or insight arises (or drops in), and the teacher knows what is needed to help the child. It is interesting to note that this happens most frequently when we seek answers for another's need. Most of the time we do not recognize that we have received insights, but think that we are insightful. We think how clever we are; "I am such a great teacher; look how I can come up with all the best solutions for my class." This can occur in many situations. We may be presenting a lecture to others, and say something new that we did not know before in response to another's question. The insight lands in us during the lecture. Those who are aware of the help we receive do recognize where the insight came from; others do not, and may feel proud of their lecturing skills.

Many people receive inner pictures that they respond to without knowing that they have been given to us through the capacity of our unbound soul powers being open to receiving them. When we don't recognize that we have received an imagination, our own ego claims it. Not only does this lack of recognition separate us from the guiding spirit (because the spiritual law states that the more we recognize the spirit, the more it may work with us); but also it increases our egotism, our self-love, which also divides us from the spiritual whole.

When we recognize where the insights come from, we develop a closer relationship to the helping spirits, and we begin to recognize their consistent connection and guidance shining light into our inner life. We recognize the superiority of these wisdom-filled thoughts. "We attach little importance to our own thinking; we regard it as something inferior compared with the thoughts pouring into us from the cosmos, which are interwoven with the divine."[53]

If they are recognized as helping powers, in time the light of these insights can begin to develop into a deep inner gratitude. Instead of "I'm so great," we feel grateful. It is this gratitude, not a false pretense of gratitude, but rather a true upwelling of gratitude from our being, which allows the imagination, the gift, to continue its work inwardly. It does not stop at the level of an insight, but penetrates more deeply into our etheric body. When a spiritual insight penetrates into our etheric body through our gratitude, it begins changing the streaming movements of our own inner rhythms of life. All that was dull or washed out begins to stream, in connection to the incoming impulse. Slowly, in time, it begins to bring us into rhythm, into the harmony of life-giving spiritual consciousnesses. We become more related to the spiritual beings that work with us. Over time, this changes us. The etheric body slowly changes from a familial relationship with the earthly community and family to a familial relationship to the higher consciousnesses.

Through these inner changes, we may feel, on one hand, more truly engaged with concerns for humanity, because this is the concern of these divine beings, and why they help us. On the other hand, we can feel even greater isolation than before, because more of our inner being is considering life and our human task in such a different way from the common way. We are left with a feeling of being "in the world, but not of the world." We begin to recognize how conditioned to being asleep much of humanity is; how many are separated from a true relationship to the spiritual community and, therefore, from their own essential selves. They are fighting over broken toys, instead of using the marvelous opportunity of life.

True Clairaudience

The intellectual soul (which is bound primarily to the etheric body, and has an intimate relationship with what formed the etheric body from the spiritual world) becomes for the spirit the *Inspirational Soul.* This allows for the spirit to perceive the world of spiritual activities and powers, which are behind the pictures or imaginations, and produce them. They give the capacity to read what is seen and to understand its deeper meaning. In the sense world, seeing lines on a page is not enough to understand the meaning of the lines. The meaning lives not only in the word; it is how the word is used and where it is used that allow us to read correctly the picture another is conveying. Reading spiritually is accessing the meaning or intention behind the pictures that are seen. The meaning has a power or activity that we are moved by. It has a life or a motion that is experienced in the spiritual world as a reverberation or sounding. The capacity to perceive the sounding is spoken of as a kind of hearing, although no ear is required. This is a capacity that can be developed by the few who are initiated into this world of spirit life.

The intellectual soul, on this side of the threshold in everyday life, mediates the inspirations given from the spiritual beings. Receiving inspirations is different from receiving imaginations. Inspirations come with the power, the force, to do what has been perceived as needing to be done; we are moved into action by it. We feel invigorated, fortified, and energized to carry out what is needed.

When we speak to another out of this inspiration, we pass on the power to the other. In us and through us, the spiritual world can serve the outer world. When we speak out of our personal intellect, others receive intellectual pictures and whatever association they can bring to it, like the child learning about nature from a screen. If we speak from a place of spiritual inspiration, others feel strengthened and fortified, as though they have encountered the experience directly in themselves. Such an encounter often results in others feeling inspired or uplifted, so that they have the courage to meet what faces them.

When we give lessons that we are inspired by, not only are we not drained, but neither are the recipients. True spiritually-inspired speaking always leaves us strengthened. It may not be accompanied by complicated spiritual pictures, as one might presume. The thought that is communicated may actually be simple, but it is imbued with a spiritual power that has its own strength and health-giving rhythm.

This healing force that is directly given through inspiration can penetrate very deeply into the one who receives this from the spiritual world. It does not have to stop at invigorating the etheric forces, but can continue right into our physical bodies. This health-giving power can bring some necessary adjustments. We may experience these adjustments in our physical health for a while. Often these seem like sickness, because the changes can bring about symptoms such as headaches or disturbances in the rhythm of the heart, as well as a range of pains or sensations in the body; but they generally settle quickly.

Steiner gave the example of a child living in a polluted city who may feel sick at first when being taken into the fresh mountain air. This does not mean the air is bad for him; but the clearing produced by the clean air is uncomfortable. The experience of being changed by what we have received can leave us feeling that we are configured differently from others, even though there are no outward signs. Inwardly these changes could give rise to another level of separation and isolation from our fellow human beings. If we are not careful to work consistently with the uniting force of the spirit, we might be tempted to remove ourselves from others.

True Clairsentience

The sentient soul (which is bound to the astral body and to the laws of the astral world) becomes for the spirit the *Intuition Soul* on the other side of the threshold. To begin with, the astral or soul sheaths that have not been transformed into spiritual organs must first be surrendered into the soul world. Anything that has not been taken hold of by the spirit cannot enter the spiritual world. This surrender allows the soul to expand into the widest spaces of endless consciousness. Although this is often one of the first profound experiences in the preparation toward crossing the threshold (and therefore the one most commonly described), it alone does not reveal the presence of other consciousnesses. This experience is part of the initiation preparation, and can be achieved through certain practices that are given as contemplations in this chapter.

The soul once surrendered into the astral world retains only the I-consciousness, the eternal self, and the parts of the soul that have been spiritualized into the imagination soul, inspiration soul, and intuition soul, which are now the eternal soul. The I is the part of our being that belongs to the spiritual world, and is a citizen of that world, although it cannot benefit from it without the transformed soul sheaths providing the organs of perception. Just as living in the physical world requires organs of perception, so does living in the spiritual world. However, unlike the physical organs that are given to us without our effort, we must cultivate the spiritual organs ourselves. All that was not transformed into spiritual organs must dissolve back into the soul world, because it is still of that world. Only the transformed parts of the soul journey onward across the threshold, because they have become spirit substance.

The intuition soul (or transformed sentient soul) now may unite with the being of other beings in the spiritual world. Life of the soul in thought will gradually widen through initiation to a life of spirit beings.

It is through the transformed sentient soul that we can unite with others in our earthly life. It allows us to unite our core consciousness of self with another on this side of the threshold, and to stay present to the experience. In our lifetime many people can achieve this, and it can be developed by those working on the inner path. To be able to unite our consciousness with the consciousness of others goes even deeper than empathy or compassion, because we are becoming one with what lives in other beings. This means experiencing their pain as not separate from myself, but as though the other is my other self. We can learn to be in the skin of the other, whether it is a rock, plant, animal, or person. We can extend our consciousness so that there is no division between our consciousness and the consciousness of the other; there is no division between my being and the being of the other. It is as though I live in them and they live in me. This inner reality begins to change our deeds toward others, toward the world. Hafiz speaks of this change in his poem "I have come into this world to see this":

> I have come into this world to experience this: women
>   and men so true to love they would rather die before
>   speaking an unkind word,
> Women and men so true their lives are His covenant,
>   the promise of hope.
> I have come into this world to see this;
> The sword drop from men's hands even at the height
> Of their arc of rage
> Because we have finally realized, we have finally realized,
> There is just one flesh we can wound.[54]

Through the transformation of these three soul sheaths into spiritual soul organs the initiated I becomes aware of various realms of spirit consciousness. Through these soul capacities being developed and used on the earthly side of the threshold, life becomes richer, deeper, and whole again. An individual may develop very far in this direction without being called up to the I-initiation. We know that we are connected to the living spiritual world through the doorway of the transformed soul sheaths; and we live more and more consistently with this wellspring of life.

In each human being we can recognize transformed and untransformed soul processes. Developing these first spiritual soul capacities does not mean the work stops; but it may mean there is more to give the world. Here is a verse that can work toward our passing on to others in need what we have received.

I descend into the deepest soul forces within me,
Where I live and feel in my eternal soul.
As the point contracted in the circle,
Is the eternal soul without physical being within me.

With this bodiless, eternal being I think,
Helping in spirit of _____ [say name, while holding the image of the person's higher being in your consciousness, then address the person inwardly with these words]
Power to be yourself, let it grow stronger in you;
Light shining in your core, let it live livelier in you;
Soul warmth streaming from your own spirit, let it warm you through.[55]

The transformed part can be recognized by three qualities that seem to flow naturally from the one who has them. They are: a deep interest in other human beings, through the recognition of the divinity of each person; an experience of freedom in our religious life and social conditioning; and an unquestionable insight into the spiritual nature of the world. It requires a strong soul power to bear these qualities into a world that opposes them.

The Preparation

Our relationship to the non-sense perceptible worlds is an individual one, simply because of what we individually carry with us. The three soul sheaths are developed differently and to different degrees in each person. It is extremely rare for all three to be transformed equally before this stage of inner work. The many lives we have lived have created particular capacities in every area of our inner life. Although the ideal path of development may be described in the schooling, no one walks it in an ideal way.

Behind the veil of the physical world lie the living consciousnesses of the spiritual world. All that is experienced in the spiritual world is experienced as living thought beings, consciousnesses. We may think this to be an illusion, but in reality this experience reveals to us the illusion of the external transitory world. The first glimpse of this illusion is the beginning of the preparation toward the initiation of the I.

We all enter into this world of the spirit through the gate of death. When we leave this life, first we lay down the physical body that belongs to this mineral existence; and then the etheric body is surrendered to the elemental world. This surrendering takes approximately three days after the death of the body. The soul, released from its state of being body-bound, perceives images in picture form of the life it has led, expressed in the elemental world. These elemental pictures continue to unfold until all has been revealed to the soul. It perceives all its positive actions in life, when it helped another work in harmony with the world order; it also perceives all its negative actions in life, when it hindered another or worked against the harmony of the evolving collective consciousness.

When this panorama has been seen, and all is accounted for to the extent required for the individual soul, it may then dissolve into the astral world. All that is left, all that exists, is the true I. As a spirit among spirit consciousnesses, all that exists is this.

> I gaze into the darkness
> in it there arises a light—
> living light!
> Who is this light in the darkness?
> It is I myself in my reality.
> This reality of the I
> does not enter into my earthly life.
> I am but a picture of it
> but I shall find it again
> when with goodwill for the spirit
> I shall have passed through the gate of death.[56]

The path of initiation allows the human being to walk consciously through this gate while living in a physical body on the earth. In life there is no recall of our after-death experience; but for the initiate, that world has now become a part of the greater worlds. Initiates pass through experiences similar to what the dead experience, but initiates are awake and able to recall these experiences.

The soul of the initiate also leaves the body, as in death, but the etheric body does not dissolve in the same way. It expands and follows the path of revealing the past. The etheric body is in the elemental world and reveals the pictures of the past it has been carrying in the elemental substance, while the soul looks on.

For the individual to be ready for such experiences, the soul must be strengthened and prepared; the life it has known until now is about to become very different. The I can take into the world of spirit as organs of perception only the part of the soul that has been transformed. The rest, the personal soul, dissolves into the astral world.

When you are with everyone but me, you are with no one.
When you are with no one but me, you are with everyone.
Instead of being bound up with everyone, be everyone.
When you become the many, you're nothing empty.[57]

Before the I-initiation takes place, there are many preparatory steps. Students of the inner work can ready themselves through certain necessary schooling exercises. Such work will lead to a healthy crossing of the threshold through the initiation given by the beings of progression.

Preparations include: contemplating the pictures given in the esoteric schooling of what will be met in preparation and crossing of the threshold; developing greater courage inwardly to meet ourselves and all the light and dark that lives in us; preparing the soul to step into new transformations and experiences, rather than step away from the unknown when the moment arises.

There are three primary steps that need to be prepared for. This preparation is extremely useful even for those who will not take that step across the threshold in this lifetime. It prepares us to meet the spiritual truths that must be encountered at some point in our development. One thing we need to prepare for is meeting our past.

PREPARATION 1: Meeting the past

If we have begun the steps of self-development as described in chapter three, we have already begun this preparation in some form. For much of the time, the preparation is recognizing what still needs to be worked on. We would have seen in our self-development exercises and our meditation exercises all that still needs transforming and strengthening. This can be most clearly judged from a direct experience from an encounter with a being called the lesser guardian of the threshold. The guardian bars the way until all the necessary requirements are met in terms of seeing what lives in us and our personal particular self.

For a few, the soul encounters the guardian in the form of an etheric double that is made manifest in the elemental world. For most, we follow the truth that the non-sense perceptible worlds are experienced before they are seen. The elemental world stands between our physical perceptions in earthly life and the soul-spiritual world. Here in the elemental world all the pockets of untransformed activities of our soul are gathered together and made manifest as a separate entity that we can look upon as one would see something in the physical world; but this entity is experienced inwardly. At the same time it is a greater reality, as is the nature of the spiritual world. This is an uncomfortable encounter because we see and feel all the error that lives in us.

The elemental world can present pictures, images that have a familiar relationship to the world of sense, even though the images are not fixed as in the sense world, but rather always moving and changing. Every thought becomes a living entity that is consistently being affected by its surroundings. Not everyone will "see" into the elemental world; some may experience these events only in the inner life.

In the soul and spiritual world that lives beyond the elemental world, these sense-based pictures do not exist; but since we must use words to describe the spiritual world and the beings of consciousness, we must use pictures that belong to the world of sense, even though they are never "seen" in the same way. All that takes place spiritually is an activity of true spiritual realities, although it is always possible that the elemental world will then create an image of this reality, which will then act under the elemental laws. So the Rosicrucian admonition is an important reminder:

Guard yourself in esoteric striving from being drowned.
Guard yourself against burning your own I in the fire.[58]

We may be drowned in the overwhelming fear of the reality of the elemental world as we raise ourselves to the macrocosm. We may burn in shame at the inadequacy of our microcosmic life that is engulfed in egotism. It is the guardian itself that ignites the fear and shame that bar us from taking further steps until we are sufficiently prepared.

Meeting our past by encountering the double is not necessarily as terrible as some would expect; it depends on the transformation previously made. In time, the lesser guardian will change from admonishing about wrongdoings that need correcting to being a servant giving advance warning, and therefore preparing us for what lies ahead. However, we will always need courage to meet this being. We set the right ground with courage that we have begun developing while taking hold of our personal self on the path of self-development. Yet nothing can quite develop the courage for further development more completely than the first guardian encounter. The guardian is present in some form in all true preparation toward crossing the threshold.

PREPARATION 2: Meeting the future

Meeting the future of our progression is another necessary preparation. This is best achieved by contemplating the pictures given by the initiates of the spiritual world. There is no clearer pathway that the future human being will walk than that outlined by the initiates. This path is described in the esoteric lessons of the First Class of the School of Spiritual Science. Rudolf Steiner present-ed these nineteen lessons as one part of the necessary preparation that the soul must go through. Through en-countering these pictures in the earthly world, the soul is developed inwardly; but more important, the soul may carry the wisdom of the spiritual content as inner wis-dom across the threshold. Only that which is a spiritual truth may continue into the spiritual world and be help-ful. All other self or personal pictures are lost in order not to influence a clear seeing. These true pictures, which we ensoul as a preparation, in the form of mantric verses of the class work (or which are imparted by the guard-ian directly to the candidate for initiation) become the guideposts and directions that are required to meet the various spiritual experiences. The pictures also become as magnets to the spiritual consciousnesses that resonate with them. They act as guidance and support.

If we can immerse ourselves in them, these soul pictures stay with us as living activities. They prepare us for all the likely steps that will be met in our preparation to cross the threshold. One of these is an encounter with the three beasts. These three need to be encountered, even if the individual has transformed the personal shadow aspect of soul. All humanity is called to encounter the collec-tive shadow of the collective soul of our times, which the beasts represent.

We all are vulnerable to these three powers, which serve as the shadow of our times and bar the way forward in our relationship to living spiritual activity. They are the accumulated forces of the collective soul; and yet they affect us individually, sometimes to the extent that we are blocked entirely in our lives from having any relationship at all to the spiritual world. Most of us have encountered these three beasts as they appear in our lives in more subtle ways: doubting what is experienced inwardly; hating what is revealed to us about what lives in us; or fearing what will become of us as we progress beyond the small self.

The three beasts rise up out of the abyss that divides the sense world from the spiritual world. They are called the three beasts of the threshold, and at this stage of development we must come to know them in their true form. These three distortions are the negative counterpart of our soul forces of thinking, feeling, and willing.

These beasts reveal themselves not only in the elemental world and on the threshold to the true spiritual world, but also in our inner life. They live not only as thoughts that cross our mind, planting seeds that can undermine us; but also as forces that assail us. They can be described in pictures, or as an activity such as we experience as dull blue, washed-out yellow, and dirty red. If, instead, we experience purified soul forces illuminated by the I as inner qualities, the living colors would be experienced as shining blue, radiating yellow, and vibrant red.

The beasts will be inwardly "seen" only if the elemental world forms the picture and the individual has access to seeing into the elemental world. The soul qualities of these beasts are doubt, hatred, and fear. However, in the world of living thought-beings, these forces are not flat intellectual concepts, but living activities that can feel like an assault if encountered. The doubt, the hatred, and the fear that we must encounter are not what lives in us toward the outer earthly world, but what lives in us expressed toward the spiritual world itself. These forces live in our own thinking, feeling, and will; and now in the inner world they reveal themselves as they are. What is of importance is that we gather the strength to confront the experience of their power and pass beyond their grasp, which prevents us from stepping further.

The development of capacities that have been transformed in each soul sheath will determine the face of the beast that will meet us. The development of the three soul sheaths will also determine the capacities to perceive clearly these three beasts as separate from ourselves.

The first beast is fear in our will. Fear of what the spirit wills for us causes the elemental world to rise as a nightmare in our consciousness. The way to overcome this is through the courage we have developed along the path, and the great hope that we can cultivate toward the guiding spirit beings and the path we walk toward true spiritual knowledge.

The second beast is hatred in our feeling. Hatred hollows out our inner life as it repels the supporting powers of the soul; we can feel flattened and discouraged. We may hate what the divine revelation reveals about us; and the power of the divine pulls back from our hatred. We need to counter this hollowing out through our love toward the divine-spiritual world and our fiery enthusiasm toward the path of evolving humanity.

The third beast is doubt; we doubt spiritual experience. What will we become if we are diminished into nothing? In doubt we are severed from the creative force of spirit being. Thoughts of doubt in the spiritual world rock the soul at the root of our being. Doubt creates an inner split in the consciousness, which causes division within and an internal battle. We begin to look for solid material convictions about what is true and real. We doubt what we have experienced inwardly; we doubt the path and the work of the initiates. Faith in the spirit working in our lives expels the doubt; knowledge of the spiritual world that has been passed through esoteric teachings and has become our own knowledge expels the doubt.

The guardian not only prevents premature entry across this threshold, but also directs and prepares us for the crossing, guiding us in the overcoming of the three beasts. As difficult as the admonishments of the guardian are, they serve to awaken us in full freedom to our relationship with the spiritual world. The guardian works on behalf of the good of all humanity.

PREPARATION 3: Meeting the present

The soul must learn to relinquish everything that is the personal, particular self. First, students are able to take the steps of seeing all their shortcomings. What needs to be transformed shows itself, perhaps even through the mirror of the elemental world. Then, after recognizing the three soul activities that need to be overcome and balanced through the strength of the individual, all that is left of the personal being must be dissolved into the soul world. Only the spiritual forces of the three soul sheaths may remain, because only these have a constructive purpose in the spiritual world.

The next preparation of the soul, therefore, is to develop its capacity to extinguish all that still is itself, all that gives it its particular singular experience. Through the previous stages of development and meditation, the soul has developed a concentrated experience of self-awareness, which is able to hold itself as a point in the vast consciousness. The stronger the soul, the clearer its perceptions will be.

The soul now works to be capable of dissolving itself. In order that the true I may arise, the particular self must dissolve.

> Whatever is singular, particular, and individual must find the spirit in itself. Human beings feel and know themselves as individuals when they awake to full consciousness. This leads us to overcome our particularity; it allows spirit to live in us; and allows us to conform ourselves to the spirit. In and from ourselves, we must rise up and cast off all that is selfish, all that makes us this particular individual being; for this particular is what darkens the light of the spirit.[59]

To overcome particularity, the student needs to find a new relationship to the present. Being nothing in the present is the other preparation. For some, this preparation may be the hardest task to work on; and yet it may be easier for others. The soul must become accustomed to being nothing, to being just a point in the vast consciousness of the spiritual world. We train for this state of nothingness in the meditative practice through extinguishing all that is built up in the exercises.

However, there are several exercises that specifically prepare the soul for this necessary annihilation in the way it will now need to ready itself, so that what is transformed may cross the threshold. If it is not prepared, the soul will pull back at this point until it can trust in its capacity for surrender. The student may well need to have a meditative practice for these deep contemplations to be fruitful; they have been included here because many students of the inner work get stuck at this point. Through our understanding of the exercises, we can discern where we are in our practice. These exercises can also be useful for students who find that through meditative practice they can achieve empty consciousness, but they experience the inner space as though they are in a dark empty room; or for others who may experience this nothingness as a profound abyss of darkness.

This preparation leads to the portal of the experience of the true I. While we live in the body, the body-self is dominant. When we pass into the world of soul, the soul-self is dominant; now leaving the soul world behind, we may meet the true I. This extinguishing has sometimes been called the midnight hour of the soul (or the dark night of the soul), when all has to be released and nothing is left. There needs to be nothing of me, no selfness, so that the true self, the true I may reveal itself.

Here are six contemplations that speak to the three different strengths of the soul and are pointing to the same spiritual experience. They have the capacity to help individuals prepare right up to the point where they can be called across the threshold through their individual destiny.

These contemplations are given to enhance our understanding and clarify the journey. It is not suggested that they be taken as a meditative practice by themselves. However, for those who have a firm meditative life, and for those who already have encountered these inner experiences, the following may be vital for further recognition of where each sheath is working, and therefore for further progression.

It is useful for the student to compare these exercises, both through your own experience of them and by evaluating what they offer. As contemplations they require long and attentive consideration and concentration within our being. All such spiritual matters are worthy of our contemplative time. Each of the six exercises is a separate practice and needs individual attention; however, much is learned about the path and ourselves by comparing and evaluating their different effects.

CONTEMPLATION 1

What is it to disappear and rise again
out of one's disappearance?

CONTEMPLATION 2

How does the point become a circle,
and the circle a point?

Signs or symbols work profoundly on the soul, partly because they bypass the intellect, but also because they are closer to soul language. For these contemplations, hold the one symbol in the center of your consciousness, not as a picture in front of you, but as a sign within your center. Avoid placing the sign in the body. Place it in the center of your consciousness, as the only thing that exists.

CONTEMPLATION 3

Involution is the contraction of spirit in the soul's interior. Evolution is the expansion of spirit outside the material.

No evolution is possible without the corresponding and simultaneous involution.
No involution is possible without the corresponding and simultaneous evolution.

CONTEMPLATION 4

Contemplate how the point becomes a sphere yet remains itself. Then you have grasped how the infinite sphere is still a point; and you will see how the infinite can appear as finite.

CONTEMPLATION 5

As human beings we are a stage where the eternal and the transitory meet.

Our knowing is an experience of the eternal, for which we ourselves are the organs of cognition.

Our action is the action of the eternal, for which we our-selves are only mediators.

Understand therefore:

You are the primal spirit's eye; through you this spirit
sees creation.
You are the primal spirit's hand; through you the spirit
creates.

CONTEMPLATION 6

The germ of my body lay in the spirit.
And the spirit incorporated into my body
Sensory eyes,
That I might see through them
The light of bodies.
And the spirit stamped my body
With sensation and thought
And feeling and will
So that through them I might perceive bodies
And work on them.
The germ of my body lay in the spirit.

The germ of the spirit lay in my body
And I will incorporate in my spirit
Suprasensory eyes
So that I might see the light of spirits.
And I will stamp my spirit
With wisdom and power and love
So that the spirits may work through me
And I become the self-conscious instrument
Of their deeds.
The germ of the spirit lies in my body.[60]

All these six exercises prepare the soul for transiting across the threshold by extinguishing all that is not I. But they do so in different ways. It is useful to see which exercises speak to you; to recognize which of the exercises seem most familiar. Which are easier to grasp? Which of the exercises seem alien? Observe which exercises achieve immediate experience, and which are difficult to gain any experience from until they are worked with in deep contemplation.

Guiding Beings and Diverting Beings

Through certain techniques, such as breathing exercises or substance use, it is quite possible for us to take the undeveloped and un-strengthened soul sheaths across a threshold; but this is not the same threshold that is watched over by the guardian. This diverted astral threshold leads us, not to the free and true relationship to the spiritual world and the beings of progression, but rather to a partial relationship to the spiritual world. The soul accesses partial pictures, partial activities, or partial beings. This will always lead to some form of distortion and disturbance to the soul. For the soul that sees only part of the truth, either the desire to leave the earthly world becomes immense or the desire emerges to make the spiritual world another earthly experience, making it like this physical existence. The crossing via the guardian of the threshold, which involves a conscious grappling with ourselves, is a sure sign of crossing in the ways of the progressive beings.

Entering these next pictures that describe the divine and diverting consciousnesses is not easy for some people. This is not only because the beasts bar the way through fear, hate, and doubt, but also because of an individual's past; perhaps, for instance, because of religious conditioning some have a block toward the spiritual world. If we can penetrate these words by Rudolf Steiner—given here once again—they may serve to reduce our reaction, "It is well never to lose sight of the fact that fundamentally all that exists is consciousness, consciousnesses. Anything outside the consciousness of beings of whatever order belongs to the realm of maya, the great illusion."[61]

Not all higher spiritual beings work on behalf of the progress of humanity. If we were to picture the consciousness that lives behind human egotism and the desire to serve ourselves, then the being we would perceive is one that is named by many esoteric schools as Lucifer, or the hosts of luciferic beings that serve this consciousness. Luciferic beings want humanity to cross the threshold prematurely; they tempt us with a life that separates us from the collective strivings of humanity. They lure us to escape the responsibilities of daily life for the bliss of spiritual elevation. The desire to abandon the earth's evolving for the soul's own satisfaction and gratification indicates the egotistical grip. This great temptation is intended to draw souls out of the evolving stream of time.

These consciousnesses tempt human beings to cross the threshold into the spiritual world before they are ready, taking their untransformed selves with them; they lead us into Lucifer's domain in the astral world. This is the case with wanting to gain spiritual insight for power over others, power for self-gain. This leads to all sorts of illusions about the spiritual world, because whatever we take with us alters what we can perceive. In this situation, the effects will not be a soul that is unable to relate to the outer world; but, rather, a soul that is disturbed by the premature crossing and ends up with a disorder, or egotism that goes beyond the normal bounds, such as megalomania. All conditions of this disturbed nature prevent further development in that particular incarnation, although the individuals themselves may be entirely unaware of their condition. They may even believe in themselves so much that they set themselves up as gurus of the path, feeding their need to be special.

If we now turn our attention toward the consciousness that lives behind materialism, we find the activity of beings that come under the rule of Ahriman. The ahrimanic beings work in a different way from the luciferic beings; they are the consciousnesses behind materialistic thought and our belief in our separate selves. They wish to hold spiritual development back, and allow us to experience only as far as the elemental world. This gives the illusion that the spiritual world is similar to the physical world. The so-called spiritualists who connect with the dead, telling people about the other side in such earthly terms, are operating out of this elemental world. Here the shell of the departed soul still resides, and continues to express itself in changing pictures. The spiritualist can amplify the greatest materialism by working out of the elemental world.

The changing pictures are laws of the elemental world. It is not the individual soul that spiritualists connect with, but a shell of the soul. The soul shell or the etheric shell that was left in the elemental world has memory pictures of the past incarnation. This is what makes us believe we have contacted the real being who has crossed the threshold; whereas we have merely contacted the memory pictures of the shell.

Ahrimanic consciousness and its minions overpower human progression through us if we believe that all that really exists, or is important, is the physical world. These beings wish to sever humanity by drawing it downward; they use the human being's capacities and powers for their own aims. We exhaust our powers in the futile activity of concentrating on our material life alone, even if it is in the guise of spiritualism.

The higher I is the doorway to the progressive beings of the spiritual world. The higher I, like all our sheaths, has its spiritual counterpart, meaning there is a spiritual being behind the sheath. They are made from the same substance; the spiritual being carries the whole, while the individual carries the part; yet they are not separated. In this schooling, the name Christ is given to identify the being or consciousness that carries the whole; whereas the phrase higher I is the name for the part. The angels, archangels, and archai are some of the names given to the consciousnesses that work to serve this higher I, and have progressed themselves on this path.

Through the initiation of the I, the part will be initiated into the whole, and we will come to know directly these consciousnesses ourselves. There are no shortcuts; something has to be surrendered to know the truth. "If we bring ourselves into relation, let us say, with an angel or an archangel being of the spiritual world and want to gain some ideas concerning that being; that is, if we want to perceive that being truly, we must first destroy something in ourselves."[62] Some do not know this consciousness by the name Christ; they may call it by some other term that names their own spiritual ideal. Whatever name they give the being in their experience, all agree it is the Being of Love.

All human beings have a doorway for all three spiritual beings to be active within them. We can sometimes detect them when trying to make a decision. One pulls us upward into self-preservation; "I am everything" is its temptation. The other pulls us downward toward a purely outer existence; "I am nothing" is its fight. Between them as a balance is a Being of Love: "I am." The "I am" presents a possibility that we may choose to follow or not. The Being of Love does not pull us, but leaves us free.

Each of us has the divine spark, the highest connection to the spirits of progression; each has its selfness and egotism that links us to the luciferic forces acting in the soul; and each has the material forces of the ahrimanic consciousness that connect us with the outer bodily world. All are necessary for us to work and to develop as human beings. Therefore all must continue to exist. The essential question is, who governs? The life in the body and soul has thus far served the spirit, to awaken our conscious relationship to it. It is now through the spirit that we find our freedom. Through the power of the spirit we may transform the human soul and body, and redeem the diverting forces.

> I want to fire everyone
> with the spirit of the cosmos
> so each becomes flame
> and unfolds the fiery being
> of their being.
>
> Others would rather
> draw water from the cosmos
> to quench the flames,
> to douse the inner
> spark of all being.
>
> Oh joy when the human flame
> is incandescent even at rest.
> Oh bitterness when a wretched soul
> is bound, held back from rousing itself.
>
>   – Rudolf Steiner[63]

Those who live in the spirit live free; they recognize the truth and reality of spiritual life. The higher I, being now the mediator between the individual and the higher spiritual beings, is able to impart the way of living and being that serves the progression of humanity. It is only through the living spirit that the progressive path is carved.

To will as a separate being is to be a worthless point at the periphery of the universe, disappearing in the stream of time. To will in the spirit is to be at the center, for then the center of the universe resurrects you. If you act as a separate being, you lock yourself out of the closed chain of world action; you cut yourself out. If you act in the spirit, you live into universal world action.[64]

At any point, the human being is susceptible to impressions, insights, and thoughts that stream from either progressive beings or diverting beings. Without the foregoing preparation, it would be hard for us to perceive this consciously. The human being is constantly in a state of inner warfare; our inner life is not separated from this spiritual battle between the good and malevolent beings. The only reason an individual would walk this path is to ensure that what comes in and through the individual as a mediator of the heavens and the earth is connected to the progressive beings.

Only through this awakened free consciousness can we be sure that what we do is for the good, and that it streams from the creative forces of the universe. We can never see the whole picture. An action today may be good in the chain of the world-all; the same action tomorrow may be malevolent, extending from self-gain. We know this to be true from experience in our own lives.

Through our living connection to the spiritual world and the beings of progression, we can recognize the good. It is our free choice, and it must be our free choice, whether or not we do the good. To perceive what is right and true is easier than living what is right and true. Just like the hard work of self-transformation, we can perceive what needs transforming; we can feel it needs to be done, but can we do it?

These three possibilities of our direct living relationship to the spiritual world become for the world a spiritual deed, not a personal one. We learn to perceive what is true, to connect ourselves with the truth, and then to live the truth. All three together become a deed of love toward the world. It is love because we are free to act, or not to act. It is love because when we give of ourselves the very forces that we could have used for ourselves stream out behind the deed toward the other. It is love because we could pass it by; but instead we take it upon ourselves to work the good work, knowing that the future that is being prepared by the divine beings is also in our own hands.

Notes

Introduction

1. Rudolf Steiner, *Reincarnation and Karma: Two Fundamental Truths of Human Existence* trans. D.S. Osmond, C. Davy, and S. and E.F. Derry (Great Barrington, MA: SteinerBooks, 2001).

2. Rudolf Steiner, *The Fall of the Spirits of Darkness,* trans. Anna Meuss (London: Rudolf Steiner Press, 1993).

3. Rudolf Steiner, *Metamorphoses of the Soul: Paths of Experience,* Volumes I and II, trans. C. Davy and C. von Arnim (London: Rudolf Steiner Press, 1983).

Chapter 1

4. Mabel Collins, *Light on the Path* (Quest Books, 1970).

5. Hafiz, *A Year with Hafiz,* trans. Daniel Ladinsky (NY: Penguin Group USA Inc., 2010).

6. Rudolf Steiner, *Six Steps in Self-Development: The Supplementary Exercises,* trans. by Matthew Barton (Forest Row, Sussex, UK: Rudolf Steiner Press, 2010).

7. Hafiz, *The Subject Tonight is Love: 60 Wild and Sweet Poems of Hafiz,* trans. Daniel Ladinsky (NY: Penguin Compass, 2003).

8. From an esoteric lesson given by Rudolf Steiner in 1923.

9. Ibid.

10. Rudolf Steiner, *Metamorphoses of the Soul: Paths of Experience.*

11. Jalal al-Din Rumi, "Checkmate," *The Essential Rumi,* trans. Coleman Barks (NY: Penguin Group, 1995).

12. From an esoteric lesson given by Rudolf Steiner in 1923.

13. Rudolf Steiner, *A Way of Self-Knowledge and The Threshold of the Spiritual World,* (Great Barrington, MA: SteinerBooks, 1999).

14. Rudolf Steiner, *The Fall of the Spirits of Darkness.*

15. Rudolf Steiner, *The Work of the Angels in Our Astral Body,* trans. A. Muess (Forest Row, East Sussex, UK: Rudolf Steiner Press, 2006).

16. Rudolf Steiner, *The Fall of the Spirits of Darkness.*

17. Rudolf Steiner, *The Work of the Angels.*

18. Rumi, *The Essential Rumi.*

CHAPTER 2

19. Jalal al-Din Rumi, "Checkmate," *The Essential Rumi.*

20. Rudolf Steiner, *Soul Economy and Waldorf Education,* trans. Roland Everett (Great Barrington, MA: Anthroposophic Press, 2003).

21. Ibid.

22. Ibid.

23. Rudolf Steiner, *The Christ Impulse and the Development of Ego-Consciousness,* trans. C. von Arnim (Forest Row, East Sussex, UK: Rudolf Steiner Press, 2014).

24. Rudolf Steiner, *How to Know Higher Worlds: a Modern Path of Initiation,* trans. Christopher Bamford (Hudson, NY: Anthroposophic Press, 1994).

25. Rudolf Steiner, *The New Spirituality and the Christ Experience of the Twentieth Century,* trans. P. King (Hudson, NY: Anthroposophic Press, 1990).

26. Rudolf Steiner, *Soul Economy.*

27. From an esoteric lesson given by Rudolf Steiner in 1923.

28. Rudolf Steiner, *Soul Economy.*

29. Rudolf Steiner, *The Kingdom of Childhood: Introductory Talks on Waldorf Education,* trans. Helen Fox (Hudson, NY: Anthroposophic Press, 1995).

30. Ibid.

31. Rudolf Steiner, *Metamorphoses of the Soul: Paths of Experience.*

32. Rudolf Steiner, *The Heart of Peace: Meditations for Courage and Tranquility,* trans. Matthew Barton (Forest Row, East Sussex, UK: Sophia Press, 2012).

Notes

CHAPTER 3

33. Rudolf Steiner, *Guidance in Esoteric Training*, trans. various (Forest Row, East Sussex, UK: Rudolf Steiner Press, 2001).

34. Ibid.

35. Rudolf Steiner, *Metamorphoses of the Soul: Paths of Experience*.

36. Rudolf Steiner, *Start Now! A Book of Soul and Spiritual Exercises,* ed. Chris Bamford (Great Barrington, MA: SteinerBooks, 2004), p. 46.

37. Ibid.

38. Rudolf Steiner, *World of the Senses and the World of the Spirit,* trans. Johanna Collis (Forest Row, Sussex, UK: Rudolf Steiner Press, 2014).

39. Ibid.

40. Mabel Collins, *Light on the Path*.

41. Rudolf Steiner, *Metamorphoses of the Soul*.

42. Rudolf Steiner, "The Mission of Truth," Lecture 3, *Metamorphoses of the Soul,* Vol. I.

43. Rudolf Steiner, *Start Now!* p. 46.

44. Rudolf Steiner, "Overcoming Nervousness," in *Anthroposophy in Everyday Life* (Hudson, NY: Anthroposophic Press, 1995).

45. Rudolf Steiner, "The Mission of Reverence" in *Love and Its Meaning in the World,* trans. various (Hudson, NY: Anthroposophic Press, 1998).

46. Ibid.

47. Frances of Assisi, in *Love Poems from God Twelve Sacred Voices from the East and West,* Daniel Ladinsky trans. and ed. (NY: Penguin Group USA Inc., 2002).

48. Rudolf Steiner, *The Effects of Esoteric Development,* trans. Jann Gates and C. Bamford (Hudson, NY: Anthroposophic Press, 1997).

CHAPTER 4

49. Rudolf Steiner, *An Outline of Esoteric Science,* trans. Catherine Creeger (Hudson, NY: Anthroposophic Press, 1997) p. 281.

50. Ibid.

51. Theresa of Avila, in *Love Poems from God Twelve Sacred Voices from the East and West,* Daniel Ladinsky trans. and ed. (NY: Penguin Group USA Inc., 2002).

52. Rudolf Steiner, *The Fall of the Spirits of Darkness.*

53. Rudolf Steiner, *The Effects of Esoteric Development.*

54. Hafiz, in *Love Poems from God: Twelve Sacred Voices from the East and West,* Daniel Ladinsky trans. and ed. (NY: Penguin Group USA Inc., 2002).

55. Rudolf Steiner, *The Heart of Peace: Meditations for Courage and Tranquility.*

56. From an esoteric lesson given by Rudolf Steiner in 1923.

57. Rumi, *The Book of Love: Poems of Ecstasy and Longing,* trans. Coleman Barks (NY: Harper Collins, 2003).

58. Rudolf Steiner, *Start Now! A Book of Soul and Spiritual Exercises.*

59. Rudolf Steiner, *The New Spirituality and the Christ Experience of the Twentieth Century.*

60. Steiner, *Start Now!*

61. Rudolf Steiner, *A Way of Self-Knowledge and The Threshold of the Spiritual World.*

62. Rudolf Steiner, "Whitsuntide in the Course of the Year," in *Art and Practical Questions in the Light of Spiritual Science,* trans. Violet E. Watkin (1955).

63. Rudolf Steiner, *The Heart of Peace.*

64. Rudolf Steiner, *The Effects of Esoteric Development.*

Bibliography

Collins, Mabel. *Light on the Path*. Quest Books, 1970.

Frances of Assisi. In *Love Poems from God: Twelve Sacred Voices from the East and West*. Translated and edited by Daniel Ladinsky. NY: Penguin Group USA Inc., 2002.

Theresa of Avila. In *Love Poems from God Twelve Sacred Voices from the East and West*. Translated and edited by Daniel Ladinsky. NY: Penguin Group USA Inc., 2002.

Hafiz. *Love Poems from God: Twelve Sacred Voices from the East and West*. Translated and edited by Daniel Ladinsky. NY: Penguin Group USA Inc., 2002.

Hafiz. *A Year with Hafiz*. Translated by Daniel Ladinsky. NY: Penguin Group USA Inc., 2010.

Hafiz. *The Subject Tonight is Love: 60 Wild and Sweet Poems of Hafiz*. Translated by Daniel Ladinsky. NY: Penguin Compass, 2003.

Rumi, Jalal al-Din. "Checkmate." In *The Essential Rumi*. Translated by Coleman Barks. NY: Penguin Group, 1995.

Steiner, Rudolf. *The Effects of Esoteric Development*. Translated by Jann Gates. Hudson, NY: Anthroposophic Press, 1997.

——. *The Fall of the Spirits of Darkness*. London: Rudolf Steiner Press, 1993.

——. *Guidance in Esoteric Training*. Various translators. Forest Row, East Sussex, UK: Rudolf Steiner Press, 2001.

——. *The Heart of Peace: Meditations for Courage and Tranquility*. Translated by Matthew Barton. Forest Row, East Sussex, UK: Sophia Press, 2012.

——. *How to Know Higher Worlds: a Modern Path of Initiation*. Translated by Christopher Bamford. Hudson, NY: Anthroposophic Press, 1994.

——. *The Kingdom of Childhood: Introductory Talks on Waldorf Education*. Translated by Helen Fox. Hudson, NY: Anthroposophic Press, 1995.

——. *Metamorphoses of the Soul: Paths of Experience,* Volumes I and II. Translated by C. Davy and C. von Arnim. London: Rudolf Steiner Press, 1983.

——. "The Mission of Truth." Lecture 3 in *Metamorphoses of the Soul*, Vol. I.

——. "The Mission of Reverence." In *Love and Its Meaning in the World*. Hudson, NY: Anthroposophic Press, 1998.

——. *The New Spirituality and the Christ Experience of the Twentieth Century*. Translated by P. King. Hudson, NY: Anthroposophic Press, 1990.

——. *An Outline of Esoteric Science*. Translated by Catherine Creeger. Hudson, NY: Anthroposophic Press, 1997.

——. "Overcoming Nervousness." In *Anthroposophy in Everyday Life*. Hudson, NY: Anthroposophic Press, 1995.

——. *Reincarnation and Karma: Two Fundamental Truths of Human Existence*. Translated by D.S. Osmond, C. Davy, and S. and E.F. Derry Great Barrington, MA: SteinerBooks, 2001.

——. *Six Steps in Self-Development: The Supplementary Exercises*. Translated by Matthew Barton. Forest Row, Sussex, UK: Rudolf Steiner Press, 2010.

——. *Start Now! A Book of Soul and Spiritual Exercises*. Edited by Christopher Bamford. Great Barrington, MA: SteinerBooks, 2004.

——. *The Threshold of the Spiritual World*. Translated by H. Collison. London: G.P. Putnam's Sons, 1922; *A Way of Self-Knowledge and the Threshold of the Spiritual World*. Great Barrington, MA: SteinerBooks 1999.

——. "Whitsuntide in the Course of the Year." In *Art and Practical Questions in the Light of Spiritual Science*. Translated by Violet E. Watkin. 1955.

——. *The Work of the Angels in Man's Astral Body*. Translated by D.S. Osmond and Owen Barfield. London: Rudolf Steiner Press, 1960; *The Work of the Angel in Our Astral Body*. Translated by A. Muess. Forest Row, East Sussex, UK: Rudolf Steiner Press, 2006.

——. *World of the Senses and the World of the Spirit*. Translated by Johanna Collis. Forest Row, Sussex, UK: Rudolf Steiner Press, 2014.

LISA ROMERO is a complementary health practitioner and adult educator, who has applied anthroposophy to her practice since 1990 and delivered education enriched with anthroposophy since 1998. Since 2006, the primary focus of her work has been teaching inner development and anthroposophical meditation. Her first book on the inner work, *The Inner Work Path – A Foundation for Meditative Practise in the Light of Anthroposophy,* was published in 2014.

Lisa lectures and presents courses and retreats on the inner work and anthroposophical meditation for professional and personal development. These are offered throughout the year in many communities worldwide. Lisa's capacity to deliver esoteric wisdom with insight and understanding allows her to meet the diverse needs of communities and professions.

For several years, Lisa was the lecturer for Health and Nutrition and Male/Female Studies at Sydney Rudolf Steiner College, where she now continues to lecture the tutors on inner development. She also designed and facilitated the Educaredo Towards Health and Healing course. This training ran eight, year-long courses working with therapists from all modalities, as well as Waldorf teachers, to bring the practical application of therapeutic and pedagogical methods. She continues to teach in numerous trainings and seminars for several organizations.

Essentially, Lisa's work springs from the inner work, meditation, and exercises, together with a dedication to the path of unfolding consciousness. She brings a depth of insight that is reflected in the experiences and changes in the participants who share in this work.

FOR INFORMATION ON COURSES AND CLASSES
CONTACT LISA ROMERO AT :

innerworkpath.com